Experiencing Exclusion

Experiencing Exclusion

Eva Pomeroy

Trentham Books

Stoke on Trent, UK and Sterling, USA

Trentham Books Limited

Westview House	22883 Quicksilver Drive
734 London Road	Sterling
Oakhill	VA 20166-2012
Stoke on Trent	USA
Staffordshire	
England ST4 5NP	

First published 2000

British Library Cataloguing-in-Publication Data
A catalogue record for this book is available from the
British Library

1 85856 228 7 (paperback)

Designed and typeset by Trentham Print Design Ltd., Chester and printed in Great Britain by Cromwell Press Ltd., Wiltshire.

Contents

For my grandmother,
Betty Kaplan Wiles

Acknowledgements

I would like to thank the staff and students at Wake Green, Link, Kings, and Burlington Behavioural Support Service Centres, whose enthusiastic co-operation made this study possible. I would especially like to thank headteachers Gwyneth Adams (Wake Green) and Nicky Martin (Link) for opening their Centres to me and incorporating me into their worlds.

I would like to acknowledge and thank Dr. Richard Hatcher and Faith Webster, Faculty of Education, UCE, for their endless support, encouragement and advice throughout this project. Their sincere interest and belief in this work has served to motivate me to continue, and their practical guidance and advice has provided the means to do so.

I would like to thank John Eggleston and Gillian Klein at Trentham Books for their interest and support in publishing this work.

Finally I would like to thank my friends and family who have supported me in so many ways in the years it took to complete this study.

List of Tables and Figures

Tables

Figures

1
Introduction

This study is based on real-life, first-hand insights – often the kind of insights that it is difficult for teachers to gain themselves, whether because of time and structural constraints or because of their necessarily more formal relationships with young people. Young people's accounts of their experiences provide essential information for teachers concerned about behavioural difficulties. The book is about the school experience of a particular group of young people – those who have been permanently excluded from school. In interviews they discussed not only their exclusion but their entire, often tumultuous experience of school. Their detailed accounts provide us with important insights into the lives of young people who experience extreme difficulty at school and may relate to other young people who have been excluded from school and also to those who are on the verge of exclusion. The picture of excluded students' experience of school presented here is derived from the young people themselves. Through their accounts we can identify features of their lives that they see as most influential in shaping their education experience: relationships with teachers, relationships with peers, schoolwork, and factors outside of school such as home life and neighbourhood peers. The qualitative approach to the study has allowed for a rich account of the interviewees' perceptions and views of their experiences.

The research is set within the context of school exclusion. Exclusion is intimately linked to disruptive behaviour. The DFE's (1992) discussion paper on exclusion states that 'exclusion of a pupil constitutes the most stringent response available to schools when faced with a serious breach of their disciplinary code' (p.1). Exclusion occurs when the young people's behaviour is deemed to be seriously inappropriate by the school. Discussion throughout this book will refer to behaviour generally rather than exclusion specifically. Behaviour, particularly disruptive behaviour, is the broad area of concern that embraces the phenomenon of exclusion. Exclusion and disruptive behaviour receive almost continuous coverage in the media. The issue is of concern to government at both national and local level.

Exclusion from school has received much attention in recent years – most probably because all evidence indicates a significant rise in the number of exclusions (*TES*, 26-9-97; *Guardian*, 22-11-96; OFSTED, 1996; Final Report to the DFE, 1995; BCC, 1995). Many commentators trace the roots of this rise in exclusion levels to the past and present governments' educational policies. Blyth and Milner (1993) comment that it is the increasing importance of school image, through league tables, that has discouraged schools from retaining disruptive students (p.263). The Children's Society cites league tables and inspections as the features of current educational policy that encourage schools to exclude unruly students in order to improve exam results (*TES*, 3-4-98). Focusing specifically on the exclusion of young people from ethnic minority groups, Bridges (1994) comments:

> It was inevitable that the Tory reforms would lead to an increase in pupil exclusions from school. Nor could it be expected that a government which declared its indifference to the potential effects of 'open enrolment' in promoting racial segregation in schools, would give the least consideration to the likely impact of its policies at the other end of the process, in schools' practices of rejecting children through exclusions. (Bridges, 1994, p.11)

The extent of school exclusion is cause for concern. In a study led by Carl Parsons, the percentage of school students permanently excluded was reported to be 0.35% in 1993/94 (Final Report to the DFE, 1995). This percentage seems relatively low but it translates into thousands of students being excluded from school. In a *Times Educational Supplement* article some months after the change of government, the number of students permanently excluded from school was reported to be 14,500 (*TES*, 20-2-98). This number is alarming in itself. It is compounded by the knowledge that the official numbers of permanent exclusions take little account of the number of students effectively excluded by unofficial means every year (Stirling, 1992).

Exclusion has a serious detrimental effect on young people, their families and society. Cohen and Hughes' (1994) study with excluded students and their families revealed that exclusion puts a strain on families because the children are home all day. They also note the added financial burden of providing an additional daily meal. Furthermore, the exclusion of one child with difficult behaviour can have a negative effect on siblings.

The Home Office reports a strong relationship between exclusion and offending. Graham and Bowling (1995) report that five of the eight female and all eleven of the male young offenders in their study had been permanently excluded from school (p.42). It is difficult to determine a causal relationship between the two, but exclusion from school certainly allows young people more time to become involved in criminal activity.

The educational consequences can also be significant. Only one in six permanently excluded secondary school students returns to mainstream school. Most of those who do not are given only a few hours home tuition each week (*Guardian*, 11-10-96). Even greater cause for concern is the Secondary Heads Association's (SHA, 1992) finding that approximately one-quarter of the excluded students in their study seemed to disappear from the system altogether (p.3). The financial cost for society is also high. In a Commission for Racial Equality study, Parsons *et al.* (1996) found that, in 1994/95, exclusions cost the education system £14 million, the police and courts £7 million, and social services £3 million (as reported in the *Guardian*, 29-11-96).

Of serious concern is the disproportionate number of students from ethnic minorities being excluded. Students of Caribbean origin are reported to be more than six times as likely to be excluded than their white counterparts (*Guardian*, 11-10-96). The disadvantage affects both young men and young women. *The Times Educational Supplement* (*TES*) reports that Caribbean girls constitute 8.8 per cent of excluded girls, although they form only 1.1 per cent of the total female school population (*TES,* 10-10-97). So the racial trends in exclusion apply to both genders even though only one-fifth of all excluded students is female (SHA, 1992). This racialisation of exclusion serves as an important backdrop to all research on exclusion from school.

Issues relating to race are interwoven throughout this book. Race features in all aspects of people's lives, particularly those from ethnic minority groups. It is not an isolated aspect of their school experience but can influence their interactions with teachers and peers, their attitudes towards school work and their lives outside of school in a wide variety of ways. This book reveals both differences and consistencies in the accounts of ethnic minority and white students. Where the accounts of ethnic minority interviewees converge, we begin to see patterns emerging of experiences that are virtually unique to ethnic minority students. For example such patterns can be found in the consideration of interaction with peers, and in the analysis of young people's engagement in their school work and the education system generally. While taking heed of racialised patterns within the school experience, it is also important to note the consistency in the accounts of young people of whatever background. When the interviewees spoke about their relationships with teachers, the social atmosphere of the school and the stresses and strains of their lives outside school, their accounts were remarkably consistent. The commonality of experience across racial groupings is notable throughout, if only because racialised patterns of experience are absent from so much of the discussion.

Although there has been considerable commentary on the issue of exclusion by the media, government bodies and educational researchers, very little of it has been derived from the views of the young people themselves. In recent years there has been a call for young people's views to be listened to carefully and incorporated into policy and practice. A Commons Education and Employment select committee recently made 27 recommendations for action to combat the number of young people not in education, training or work, one of which was that local action should be co-ordinated by forums and that these forums 'should listen to the views of young people' (*TES*, 10-4-98, p.5). Recently the Commission for Racial Equality published a good practice guide to exclusion (1997). One of their many suggestions was that pupils be involved in decision-making, particularly with respect to behaviour standards. The teachers in the study found that pupil involvement was key to co-operation and good discipline, while the young people said that being involved increased their motivation and made them feel part of the school (p.6). Clearly, the involvement of students had a positive effect for students themselves and for teachers, classrooms and schools.

These views have not been traditionally sought, however. Although researchers have taken an interest in the students' views and perceptions, their findings have rarely been employed to inform educational policy development. Yet youth perspectives are potentially invaluable to policy-makers and practitioners. For example, Sinclair-Taylor (1995) undertook a study of Special Needs students' perspectives on their school's on-site special unit. She found that the official integration policy, which had led to the placement of the unit, had not been successful in socially integrating mainstream students and those who had special needs. Young people in the special unit felt socially segregated even though they were physically integrated. School officials had assumed that the integration had been successful. It was only by speaking to the young people attending the unit that Sinclair-Taylor was able to reveal how this particular policy-in-practice failed to meet its desired outcomes (p.84). As the direct recipients of educational policy-in-practice, students possess a knowledge of the educational system that cannot be known implicitly to teachers, parents or policy-makers, as they play very different roles within the system. It is essential to gain an understanding and appreciation of this insider point of view in order to educate accurately and effectively.

Young people's accounts tell us as much about school processes and how they operate for some students as they do about the young people themselves. I am not suggesting that educational policy should be determined solely by young people, but rather that young people's views should form one of several key sources of information. Although this view is reflected by the likes of the Commission for Racial Equality it is not necessarily congruent with present government policy. A cursory glance at national newspapers will reveal that the dominant concerns in education today are school effectiveness and improvement. The establishment of league tables, OFSTED inspections and, more recently, performance-related pay all reflect the present government's concern with school effectiveness and pupil achievement. It is beyond the scope of this book to summarise the debates surrounding the School Effectiveness and Improvement Movement (see Elliott, 1996; Sammons and Reynolds, 1997; and Fielding, 1997 for discussion) but two of them are particularly relevant to this study. The first is the criticism, voiced most clearly by Rudduck et al. (1996), about the absence of student voices in discussions about school improvement. They note that pupils are the focus of school improvement in that they provide the measure of educational outputs, such as higher attainment and increased self-esteem, but that young people's views are largely ignored in the strategy development phases of educational policy. In the authors' words,

> ...pupils figure in these maps of concern as the ultimate beneficiaries but they do not feature among the people who might help to construct an analysis of the situation as a basis or determining a strategy and helping to monitor its appropriateness. (Rudduck *et al.*, 1996, p.4)

This study brings to the current debates the unique perspective of young people who have recently struggled within the educational system. The second criticism of educational policy that is especially relevant here is the criticism that present educational policy ignores the significance of student culture in shaping students' experiences. Hatcher (1998) criticises the present government's policy for failing to consider the underlying roots of racial inequality. On the School Effectiveness and Improvement Movement's attempts to tackle racial inequality, he observes that

> ...its efforts will be seriously undermined if its economic and social policies fail to tackle patterns of racial exclusion shaping the social backgrounds students come from, the labour market school prepares them for, *and the subcultures they create in response.* (Hatcher, 1999, p.276) [*italics* mine]

The present government aspires to reduce exclusions by one third by 2002 and has aimed to meet this target by decreasing the powers of schools to exclude. Recently however, they have had to make a u-turn on their exclusions policy. To appease headteachers and avoid industrial action the government has handed excluding power back to schools by curbing the power of independent appeal panels to overturn certain types of exclusions (*TES*, 4-8-2000, p.4, p.10). It is clear that simply taking away schools' power to exclude does not solve the problem of exclusion because it fails to address and redress the underlying causes of exclusion. And to understand these causes it is essential to understand the formal and informal school cultures that shape young people's experiences.

By exploring the young people's accounts of their experiences at school, this study reveals the cultures within which these students live and which shape their experiences. School culture is made up of both the formal culture of teachers and the curriculum and the informal culture created by the students. This book relates how both these cultures come to bear on the identity choices, attitudes and behaviours of students. To ignore the informal peer culture is to base policy on only partial knowledge of the educational experience of students. This study addresses the gap in current policy and provides a wide-ranging account of the experiences of a particular group of students – those who are permanently excluded from school.

The young people in this book are referred to as 'students' rather than 'pupils'. 'Students' is deemed a more appropriate term for those nearing the statutory leaving age. You will also find reference to them as 'low-status' students. Subsequent chapters show how certain school practices assign status to various students. Those deemed 'able' and 'well-be-haved' are accorded higher status by the institutions than those perceived not to have these qualities. Stanton-Salazar (1997) points out that low status is not simply the result of school processes but rather that 'social antagonisms and divisions existing in wider society' deny certain students status by virtue of class, race and gender (p.3). The interviewees in this study are overwhelmingly working-class young people who come from a variety of ethnic backgrounds. As their accounts reveal, they per-ceive themselves to be at the bottom of the formal school hierarchy, lacking the status afforded to teachers and some of their peers.

The chapters that follow tell these young people's educational stories – their similarities and their differences. These experiences are not 'levelled out' – instead the differences in their accounts are explored in depth. The similarities in their accounts will also be highlighted, parti-cularly those which tell us something about the way in which the educa-tional system operates for low-status youth. Implicit, and sometimes explicit, in the interviewees' stories are messages for that system. This book records and relays those messages in the hope that they will be acted upon to improve educational provision for all young people.

2
The Research

The young people's accounts that follow are taken from a qualitative, interview-based study of the perceptions of thirty-three excluded students about their educational experiences. They are predominantly working-class and come from different ethnic backgrounds. All have been permanently excluded from school and are attending Behavioural Support Service Centres. The study sought to explore and then offer an understanding of excluded students' perceptions of their educational experience. It tried to construct a rich and detailed account of the wide range of factors that have influenced the excluded students' experience, both in schools and Centres. Sensitive dialogue has allowed these factors to emerge and their connections to be revealed.

The researcher in the research

Research begins with researchers. It is they who construct the research question, determine the methods most suitable for exploring it, collect the data most often, conduct the analysis, interpret the data, and decide what conclusions can be drawn. The researcher is present at every stage of the research – integral to and inseparable from the study. It is essential then, before describing the study itself, to find out who the researcher is. Readers can then interpret the findings of the study from a more informed position.

I am a white Canadian middle-class woman in my late twenties doing research with an ethnically diverse, predominantly working-class, school-aged group of young men and women. My interest in this group and the issues they face is derived from the work in which I have been involved over the past nine years in 'adjunct' educational programmes. All these features of my biography and history influence my research in a number of ways. Who I am no doubt shapes the very questions I choose to ask and the answers I deem most relevant, although it is difficult to determine exactly how the biographical features integral to my identity have shaped these aspects of the research. Perhaps this is best left to the readers' interpretation.

My history of working on educational programmes provides a more transparent explanation for my interest in this study. The field in which I work is called 'development training' or 'experiential education'. The focus is personal growth and development achieved through group work and facilitated learning reviews, using as a medium mainly outdoor adventure but also the visual arts and theatre. Young people are offered the opportunity to live and work in small groups with others, problem-solve, attempt new and challenging tasks, and take responsibility for themselves and their peers. Personally I have found that the respectful, empowering approach that characterises development training is particularly effective in changing the self-perceptions, behaviours and attitudes of disaffected youth. This approach, and my experience in that field, have certainly influenced the manner in which I conduct research with young people. Familiarity with this background may also help readers to locate my views and interpretations within my personal history.

As an outsider to the field of formal education, I believe I was well-placed to elicit the views of young people who had experienced great difficulty in school. There are benefits and disadvantages to this outsider status. In my ignorance of the system, I can legitimately ask my interviewees to describe that system in their own terms and thus elicit their understanding of how it works. It may have been difficult to ask questions about the nature of the system if I was perceived to be a part of it. Consider the following dialogue:

> Eva: What's the last school you went to?
> Interviewee: Bridge End.
> Eva: Oh, where's that?
> Interviewee: Bridge End.

The benefit of enduring a somewhat embarrassing interchange is that this interviewee could have no doubt that my questions about the world in which he lives were driven by a genuine lack of knowledge, and his subsequent explanations of how that world functions were fascinating. I was also able to establish trust between the interviewees and myself relatively quickly. The young people in this study had had negative experiences of mainstream education. I believe that their perception that I was sympathetic to their stories and in no way involved with the education system helped to assure the honesty and validity of their accounts. The disadvantage of my outsider position is that I may have missed important cues or references in the young people's comments. My lack of knowledge may have cost me missed opportunities to explore certain relevant aspects of the interviewees' accounts.

My biography would no doubt have an impact on the way I was perceived by the interviewees. A concept I find useful in describing the interviewer-interviewee relationship is 'distance'. 'Distance' refers to the degree to which the interviewee perceives the interviewer to be like or unlike him or herself. Arguably, the less the distance between the interviewer and interviewee, the easier it is to foster trust, provide mutual understanding and encourage co-operation. So my being a young, white, female university student might well have influenced the amount and type of information young people chose to divulge. It was essential for me to put across my interest in understanding the experiences of all young people – not just those who were 'like' me.

I tried to be particularly sensitive to issues of race, gender and class and made every effort to communicate openness to, acceptance of, and interest in the young people's perceptions and feelings. This was my approach to the entire interview and it was particularly important in regard to race. As a member of the ethnic majority, I knew I had to demonstrate openness to understanding non-white experiences. So when, for instance, a young African-Caribbean man told me 'I hated that teacher. He was racist', I conveyed my acceptance of this claim by responding 'What did he do that made you know he was racist?' Had I said 'How do you know he was racist?' or 'Why do you think he was racist?' I would have implied a degree of doubt about his claim. Despite these efforts, I must be open to the possibility that my 'whiteness' (as well as my gender and class) may have limited both my understanding of the ethnic minority experience and the young people's willingness to share it with me.

The information about the researcher and about the methods used allows the readers to contextualise and interpret the research itself. The following sections explain how the research was carried out. Throughout the book I have included my comments along with those of the interviewees. This helps further to place the young people's comments within a context and serves as a reminder that the researcher is an integral part of the research.

Why study the views of youth?

There are two responses to this, the first relating to the way we think about knowledge and the sources of knowledge we consider to be legitimate, and the second to effective policy design.

This study is rooted in my personal belief in the inherent value of the views of young people, and a recognition that their views are often overlooked. Such a perspective finds a natural compatibility with anti-racist and feminist discourses which highlight the power imbalances that structure society. Researchers in these discourses refuse to objectify the individuals taking part in research and 'make human' the individuals in their studies. Thus, feminist and anti-racist researchers help to validate the experiences, views and perceptions of marginalised groups, regarding them as legitimate forms of knowledge. Reconsidering our sources of knowledge presents a challenge to traditional research. As Zeng (1998) observes,

> Traditionally, research has often been conducted by male, white intellectuals. Modern researchers, especially feminists, have argued that supposed rational, detached, value-free research has unconscious bias in favour of the dominant male perspective. (Zeng, 1998, p.22)

The constructed realities of 'the other', that is of individuals and groups outside the dominant group, have been too infrequently represented. The vast majority of the young people in this study experience 'otherness' by virtue of being working-class. Many also stand outside the dominant group as young women, members of ethnic minority groups, or both.

Within a society structured by power imbalances these young people find scant opportunity to express their views and, when they do, their views are easily dismissed because the way they are presented can appear uninformed and inconsistent within the context of an adult, power-holding society. However, these views should not be overlooked just be-cause their expression falls outside the conventional form within the academic forum. In my work, researching the views of young people carries with it the political aim of redressing existing power imbalances and challenging dominant views about the value of youth perspectives.

However, researching excluded students' perceptions is not simply a political activity to redress power imbalance. Understanding the per-spectives of young people is crucial to designing effective policy and developing effective teaching. As the direct recipients of educational policy-in-practice, young people's interpretation of and response to what is going on around them must be understood and built upon. There has been much research showing that young people who reject the educa-tional system, or aspects of it, express their rejection through disruption and absenteeism (Mac an Ghaill, 1996,1993; Willis, 1977; Reynolds, 1976). By blocking dialogue we are failing to educate certain young people and, equally disastrously, choking off a wealth of information that could lead to a more effective educational system. Students possess a unique knowledge of the educational system that cannot be known by the teachers, parents or policy-makers, who play entirely different roles within the system. Just as policy is informed by statistical trends and the views of involved adults, so must it be informed by the views of those most directly affected, the students.

The study

This study was conducted with permanently excluded students attending Birmingham Pupil Referral Units (PRUs). In Birmingham it is the Behaviour Support Service (BSS) that provides education for the vast majority of young people who are excluded from school. This research was carried out in four of the six Centres for secondary-school students.

Before I began the interviews I spent several days in the Centres, taking part in classes and activities. Previous experience working and conduct-ing research with disaffected youth had taught me that trust would probably be an issue and that the young people might not respond posi-tively to a stranger requesting an in-depth conversation about their educational experience. Spending time at the Centres helped the young people to get to know me and to develop a basic trust of me. This time also allowed me to become familiar with the environment in which the young people were being educated and to speak informally to them and the staff so as to gain some insight into the exclusion issues salient to all involved. Some knowledge of the relevant characters, history and practices of each Centre was useful in shaping the interview design and carrying out the research.

The initial visits totalled six days (a mix of half and full days) over February and March 1997 and included participating in Mathematics, English, Art and Life Skills classes. I was also able to exploit my experience in Outdoor Education. I took part in one Centre's Monday morning climbing sessions at the local climbing wall, and another Centre's day trip to an outdoor activity centre. Further involvement in classes and activities during June/July and September/October 1997 helped me to become acquainted with new groups of young people.

After the initial two months of informal visits, I conducted pilot interviews with four students who were permanently excluded from school. These interviews were analysed in detail and circulated amongst colleagues for comments. The pilot interviews served to provide further information about topics of particular relevance to the young people and provided a basis upon which to examine and improve the interviewing technique and refine the discussion topic areas and lines of inquiry.

Sample

I chose to focus the study on Year 10 and 11 students. Not only do they make up over 50% of all excluded school students (BSS, 1996) but their maturity and capacity for reflection contributed to fruitful data of high quality.

In my quest for an understanding of these students' perceptions of their educational experience, I wanted a sample that would capture the range of their views and experiences. I planned to achieve this by interviewing young people from each of the geographical areas of the city (North, South and Central) and by speaking to young men and women of African-Caribbean, Asian and European origins. Variation in social class within the sample was not actively sought, and all but one of the young people interviewed could be considered working-class. This classification is based on the accounts of the Heads of Centre who were asked to comment on the 'class' of the participating students. Their classification is supported by my impressionistic interpretation of the interviewees' descriptions of their family situation, type and location of residence, and their parents' occupation. Given that exclusion from school is an over-whelmingly working-class experience, class variation did not form one of the dimensions upon which the sample was selected. Rather, the young people in the study represent a range of perspectives and experiences within a working-class context.

The following tables outline the gender and ethnic breakdown of my sample, along with the ethnic and gender breakdown for all excluded students in the LEA.

Table 2.1: Ethnic and Gender Composition of the Sample

	White European	Asian	Mixed Parentage (As/Wh)	African-Caribbean	Mixed Parentage (AC/Wh)	TOTAL
Boys	13	3	1	5	1	23(71%)
Girls	5		1	3	1	10(29%)
TOTAL	18(56%)	3(10%)	2(7%)	8(24%)	2(7%)	33

This can be compared to the exclusion statistics for Birmingham over a two-year period.

Table 2.2: Exclusion Breakdown by Ethnic Origin, Birmingham

	White	Asian	Afro-Caribbean	Mixed	Unknown
1994/95	44%	12%	35%	6%	3%
1995/96	47%	14%	24%	10%	4%

(BSS, 1997)

Table 2.3: Exclusion Breakdown by Gender, Birmingham		
	Male	Female
1994/95	88.4%	11.4%
1995/96	81.4%	18.6%
		(BSS, 1997)

Collectively, the interviewees have attended thirty-two secondary schools, twenty-eight of which are in Birmingham. Of the Birmingham schools, eighteen were Community Schools, six Foundation Schools, and four Voluntary-Aided Schools. The four non-Birmingham schools included one Community School in Nottingham, a school in Halesowen whose status is unknown, one fee-paying boarding school, and one other school, the status and location of which is unknown.

Thirty-three Year 10 and 11 students were interviewed between April and December 1997, for a period ranging from 30 to 80 minutes. As the population in BSS Centres can be relatively transient, it is difficult to determine exactly what percentage of Year 10 and 11 students were interviewed. At any given time, 20-30 excluded students from these two year-groups could be attending each of the three long-stay BSS Centres. It follows that one-third to one-half of all excluded Year 10 and 11 students attending a BSS Centre during the data-gathering period were interviewed.

There was also a degree of self-selection in the sample. In adherence to the practice of the Centres, all young people involved in the study were required to obtain parental consent before being interviewed. I explained the research study to the young people, asked for their voluntary participation and provided them with parental consent forms, which they took home to be completed and then brought back to the Centre. Only students with completed forms could take part. This meant that young people whose parents did not want them to be interviewed were precluded from the study. The process of obtaining parental consent also provided the students with several opportunities not to take part if they did not wish to do so. They could choose not to bring the original form to their parents' attention or not to return a completed form to the Centre. Finally, young people with parental consent were asked on the day of the interview if they wished to take part. Two young people declined at this stage and this was respected.

It is difficult to determine the reasons why any individual or family declined to participate in the study, just as it is difficult to determine how parental/self-selection of this nature has affected the sample – although this seems negligible. The greatest effect is probably the over-representation of young women in the sample – 30% as compared to near 20% of the population as a whole in Birmingham in 1995/96 (BSS, 1997). The two young people who refused an interview were both African-Caribbean young men. This may be related to the gender and ethnic distance between the interviewer and the interviewee and is worthy of note. The resulting ethnic composition of the sample, however, is reflective of the LEA's exclusion statistics for 1995/96 (BSS, 1997).

The interviews

Semi-structured interviewing was chosen as the most appropriate method of data-collection. The complexity of the topic clearly required a sensitive, flexible and responsive method of data-collection. Further, in light of their experience of failure in school, these students might lack the motivation or ability to complete a 'pen-and-paper' exercise such as a questionnaire. The semi-structured interview allowed students the freedom to discuss their experience in their own terms while at the same time allowing me to guide the conversation to ensure that there were topics for comparison across interviews.

A number of steps were taken to construct the semi-structured interview guide. I had already spent time working with and interviewing young people excluded from school in another context. In fact, it was this experience that inspired the present study. The relevant literature was reviewed in order to highlight the salient issues already identified in the field and, as mentioned, I spent time in the Centres to gain a greater familiarity with the context, concerns and experience of the young people I wished to interview. The result is the interview framework outlined on page 18.

The interviews were framed so as to collect people's stories. The young people were asked to discuss their personal story of being at school, leaving that school and coming to a Centre. Within this framework, the

Figure 2.1: The Interview Framework

THEMATIC GUIDELINE	CONSISTENT TOPICS	ADDITIONAL TOPICS
Experience of school	Relationships with teachers	Racism
	Relationships with peers	Home life
	'Getting in trouble'	Involvement with police
	Experience of primary school	Drug use
Experience of exclusion	Control over behaviour	Changes in attitude
	Event of exclusion and related thoughts and feelings	Future plans
Post-exclusion experience	Comparisons of school to Centre	
	Attitudes towards schoolwork and education	

topics in the centre column were those often raised by interviewees as significant to their educational experience. If they did not raise one of these topics, I would initiate a question to elicit the interviewee's views. The topics in the final column were discussed only if interviewees mentioned them as relevant to their experience. Thus the themes of the conversation were consistent across interviews while the content and details varied from one individual to another.

In all interviews, I strove for an approach that treated the interviewees respectfully and helped to achieve the goal of redressing some of the power imbalances inherent in research with young people. The loose interview structure was intended to empower the interviewees by sharing control over the structure of the conversation. The content, pace and tone of each interview was largely defined by the interviewee.

Thirty-three interviews were carried out in all, producing a mass of data that was reviewed regularly during the data-collection phase. By the final phase of the data-collection in Autumn 1997, the new data seemed to be confirming and refining the existing findings rather than adding new insights – saturation point had been reached. At this point the data-collection was brought to a close and the interviews were coded and analysed. Chapters Three to Seven discuss the results of this analysis.

Concerns about authenticity

In perspectives-based research one of the key concerns is 'authenticity'. Are the interviewees actually telling you what they believe to be true? Are they being 'themselves'? In this study, several steps were taken to promote authenticity. As mentioned, I spent several days in each Centre beforehand, taking part in classes and activities so as to establish an identity that was quite distinct from that of the teaching staff and indeed, separate from the teaching profession. These visits also helped to foster a basic trust between myself and the students. Cooper (1993) comments on the importance of preliminary work of this type in perspectives-based research in schools.

> ...the researcher needs to combine ease of manner, trustworthiness and approachability, whilst presenting the image of being status worthy of the subjects' time and effort. Only if this is achieved can the researcher expect to be given the necessary access to less superficial levels of experience. (Cooper, 1993, p.326)

Establishing rapport was key in this study, where participation was voluntary. To promote further authenticity, the students were assured that the interview materials would be kept confidential, asked if they were willing to have the interview tape-recorded (one interviewee was not), and assured that any writing on the work would use pseudonyms. It was anticipated that these measures would encourage the young people to speak 'truthfully' about their thoughts and experiences.

At the outset of the project I was somewhat concerned with this issue of 'truthfulness' or the lack of it in the interviewees' stories. As the research progressed, I grew to view the issue of truth as a minor problem, if a problem at all. There was some inconsistency within the interviews, particularly concerning the chronology of events. But rather than seeing this as a lack of truthfulness, I saw it as an accurate reflection of the interviewees' experience of school. The fact is that, for many of the interviewees, memories of school are 'muddled'. This is perhaps under-standable given the amount of activity, disruptive and otherwise, that was reported as occurring on a daily basis.

There are occasions during some interviews when interviewees possibly adapted a story to create a particular image they wished to present. These occasions do not threaten the validity of the data, because they are relatively infrequent, but also because fabrication seems to be based on the details of events rather than the meanings of experiences, and it is the latter with which I am particularly concerned. For example, it is likely that one young man knowingly exaggerated the frequency of his involvement in fighting and his personal skill at it – but this does not invalidate the findings from our interview, which was that the young man's sense of self and identity was inextricably linked to physical strength and his ability to exert this strength over others. The central feature of his self-identity remains significant, regardless of the details of particular incidents he reports.

Ethical considerations

Throughout the study respectful and empowering treatment of the interviewees was a prime concern. The process began by asking young people for their voluntary participation in the study and offering several opportunities to decline. If students were not interested in taking part, they could decline passively by choosing not to return the required parental consent form, or they could state overtly that they were not interested. The passive option, in particular, offered young people an 'out' if they were not interested but did not feel comfortable about saying so.

The interview itself also aimed to be respectful and empowering. The style was interactive, providing interviewees with the opportunity to question the process. Two interviewees requested copies of the interview, either transcript or tape, and these were provided. My aim was to adopt and develop an interviewing style that was open and accepting of the young people's views and encouraged them to speak about their experiences in their own terms. The interviewees were also able to shape much of the content of the interview. This not only refers to determining topics of relevance, as discussed earlier, but also to the amount and type of information they chose to divulge. The interview questions were sufficiently open-ended to allow interviewees to disclose as much or as little as they wished. Listening to the interviewees' stories without judgement contributed significantly to redressing the power imbalance and sharing control in the research interview.

Finally, every effort has been made to protect the data. Confidentiality and anonymity were two of the agreed conditions between interviewer and interviewee before each interview began. All names have been changed – some to pseudonyms chosen by the interviewees – and measures have been taken to conceal the interviewees' identities even from the staff at the Centres who would be most likely to recognise them.

3

Exclusion, Behaviour and Identity

Introduction

Students are excluded from school as a result of engaging in behaviour that is deemed to be extremely or persistently inappropriate. Consequently, a central topic of concern for my study was behaviour. Students' understanding of their exclusion and much of their experience of school is inextricably linked to their understanding of their behaviour in the context of school. This chapter provides an introduction to the young people involved in the study and some background information about their exclusion and behavioural history. It also offers some insights into the interviewees' perceptions and understandings of their own behaviour. The chapter begins with a discussion of the interviewees' exclusion from school – the reasons behind the exclusions and the young people's responses to their exclusion. This leads on to a consideration of the interviewees' understanding of their behaviour more generally. Of particular concern is the extent to which their behaviour is viewed as reflecting aspects of their identity, or as being shaped by the situations in which they find themselves.

Exclusion from school

Exclusion is considered to be 'a last resort' (DFE, 1992, p.8) and 'the most stringent response available to schools when faced with a serious breach of their disciplinary code' (DFE, 1992, p.1). So, for what reasons are students excluded from school? The National Exclusions Reporting Service monitored all exclusions for two years commencing in Summer 1990 and concluded that 'Disobedience in various forms – constantly refusing to comply with school rules, verbal abuse or insolence to teachers – was the major reason for exclusion' (DFE, 1992, p.3). They also cite the following reasons for exclusion and how often these reasons were reported:

- physical aggression to staff: 8%

- physical aggression to pupils: 14%

- bullying: 5%. (DFE, 1992, p.3)

In the present study, reasons have been provided for 35 permanent exclusions, reported by 31 interviewees. This total is derived as follows: four of the interviewees report being permanently excluded twice, one left school before formal exclusion, and the account of another makes it difficult to determine the actual reason for his exclusion. Although the majority of interviewees reported experiencing fixed-term exclusion prior to permanent exclusion, only permanent exclusions are considered here.

The interviewees report exclusion as a result of the following:

- Sixteen of the sample describe their exclusion as the result of fighting with peers. Of these, two young people describe one significant and serious fight that resulted in their exclusion. The others describe fighting as a more pervasive feature of their experience of school. At times fighting and other forms of disruptive behaviour merge to form a multi-faceted reason for exclusion.

  Joshua: First time I got suspended, it was for wagging in my friend's house. Second time ... I was refusing to do some work for the teachers. And the third time I got suspended and then I got expelled, um that was for ... I'm not too sure what that was for. I was just messing around being naughty. I think I had a fight with some kid and I done other things and that just boiled it up so it was more than one thing for the last time.

- Seven interviewees report exclusion for their involvement in illegal activities. One was found in possession of an illegal weapon, three caused damage to, or were involved in the theft of, school property, and three were excluded for using or selling illegal substances.

- Five young people report exclusion as the result of a serious altercation with a teacher. Two of these cases include physical aggression against the teacher.

- Five interviewees report that their exclusion was the result of a variety of on-going disruptive behaviours in school. Craig summarises the accounts of this group well.

Craig: ... I dunno ... It was just...really was just, coming late, smoking, being cheeky ... being truant, arguing with the teachers. That's about it.

• Two young people cite truanting as the reason for their exclusion.

So we see a variety of reasons being cited for exclusion. For some young people the event of exclusion was significant, distinct and traumatic, and they recounted the experience in vivid detail and with great emotion. Others, such as Craig, quoted above, seem to view exclusion as one event in a long string of incidents. One senses that, for him, permanent exclusion was not a traumatic event but rather a natural conclusion to long-term, antagonistic relations between him and the school. The way in which the young people locate themselves in relation to their exclusion from school is now considered in greater detail.

Kinder *et al.* (1997) conducted a study on the perspectives of 130 students on the subject of exclusion. Forty-seven of these students had never been excluded, 64 had received fixed-term exclusions and nineteen were permanently excluded. On the basis of interviews with these students, they were able to develop a paradigm to help understand the widely varying responses of students to exclusion from school. They identify three reasons for schools employing exclusion to confront student behaviour: removal of the disruptive student for the benefit of the rest of the school, reprisal – the ultimate sanction for bad behaviour – and finally, as a remedy that would guide students to provision more suitable to them (Kinder *et al.*, 1997, p.4-8). They found that almost all the students in their study regarded exclusion as a form of reprisal. The students then locate themselves in terms of their acceptance or resistance to this reprisal. The manifest forms of acceptance and resistance are outlined on page 26.

Kinder *et al.* (1997) found that students in their study who were permanently excluded more often expressed relief/escape responses to their exclusion, regretting only the missed social opportunities (p.24). The young people in my study were more evenly divided between accepting or resisting their exclusion. The responses of fifteen interviewees would be described as 'resistance' within the paradigm outlined on page 26, most commonly in terms of relief or indifference.

Figure 3.1: Student Response to Exclusion Paradigm

Acceptance	Resistance
• distress	• fun
• concern about parental reaction	• relief
• concern about school achievement	• sense of injustice
• parental reinforcement	• feeling let down/rejected
• deprivation of social opportunities	• antagonism
• boredom	• indifference
• resolve to improve behaviour	• kudos/bravado
• wishing it otherwise/regret	• adverse effect on work (fixed-term)

(Kinder *et al.*, 1997, p.16-21)

Eva:	Can you remember how you felt?
Tonya:	I felt glad just to be out of that school.

Nahim:	Wasn't angry about being expelled.
Eva:	Oh?
Nahim:	Was angry about being in the house.
Eva:	Right. How did you feel about being expelled?
Nahim:	I didn't really care, I knew that I was expelled anyway.

Five other interviewees also mentioned that they 'knew' they were going to be excluded from school before the event whereas some of the others were shocked and dismayed when they were permanently excluded. Eleven of the young people showed signs of 'accepting' their exclusion. This was predominantly expressed through their distress.

Shelly:	I was shocked at first, but then I started becoming angry and that and started shouting at them. But I was more worried about what my dad and mum was going to say.
Leon:	I knew that moment when they arrested me that I had been expelled 'cause she goes, 'Nice having you in the school Leon', and I knew exactly from that moment that I was expelled.
Eva:	Right. Right. And how did you react to that?
Leon:	I was gutted.

Five of the interviewees described a mix of acceptance and rejection. Yvonne felt both distressed at being excluded and antagonistic towards the school for their actions in the matter. Gary said that he 'were and weren't bothered' about his exclusion, encapsulating the mix of his emotions. So the interviewees are certainly not unanimous in their responses to exclusion. We will see that their views differ on a number of fronts.

Behaviour and identity

Considering the interviewees' exclusion from school and their accounts of their behavioural history raises the broader issue of behaviour in school. Behaviour and exclusion are intimately connected. We have seen that interviewees have different responses to their exclusion. This might suggest that their views also vary on their perceptions of their own behaviour. When we look at the young people's perceptions of their behaviour we are, to a certain extent, looking at their perceptions of themselves. Behaviour reflects identity. For example, 'shy', 'wild', or 'athletic' identities all have associated behaviours. So how do the young people understand themselves in relation to their behaviour? There are two key considerations: the extent to which the interviewees' perceive themselves as deviant, and the extent to which they 'own' or feel in control of their behaviour.

The extent to which the interviewees identify themselves as delinquent or deviant can be difficult to determine. For example, Nathan describes himself and four classmates as the 'rejects' of the year, but says in the next breath:

> Nathan: I'm all right you know. I'm not that bad but there like...if I don't like somebody, I won't do it [the work] and I'll try and wreck it and everything. But if I do like it, I'll be all right with it. I'm all right.

Perhaps this discrepancy can be explained in terms of Nathan's beliefs about how he was viewed in school (as a reject) compared to his own beliefs about himself, which are reasonably positive.

Six of the interviewees describe themselves quite positively. In doing so, they seem to separate some of their behaviour from their sense of self – what they 'do' is distinct from who they 'are'.

Lorraine:	..when people in the morning go, 'Where you going?', I say, 'Oh I'm going to my Centre'. They say, 'Ooh you're bad man, you're bad'. It's me, 'No I'm not bad it's just I had a little bit of a problem'.
Leon:	Like if I think, if I'm telling someone about like what happened, then from their point of view they'll say, 'He's done a lot'. But when I think about it, I don't think, I just think I'm a normal person, you know what I mean?
Charles:	Yeah. You asked Mr. McCrae, or you know, if you ask him what Charles was like, and he'll say, 'He was a bit annoying, but he was all right'.

These young people give the impression that they understand how they are or can be viewed by others, but that they do not necessarily adopt these views as their own. Interestingly, they seem to accept the idea that some of their behaviour was inappropriate, but they do not integrate their actions into their identities. They do not seem to view themselves as 'bad' people, even if they view some of their behaviour as such. The separation between behaviour and identity distinguishes this group from another sizeable minority of the sample.

One-third of the interviewees explicitly stated that they had difficulty managing their anger. This personal characteristic and the associated behaviour seems intrinsically linked to their identity. Thus, we have interviewees who describe themselves as 'easy to wind up' or with 'a bad temper'.

Sarah:	.... you know, 'cause people know that I'm easily wound up, and like, I get annoyed really quick. That's why people always wind me up, and that's why I used to get into trouble so much.
Tonya:	...'cause I'm a short-tempered person, anybody says anything wrong, I'm out for that person...

Eva:	... So you have a temper?
Damien:	Bad temper.
Eva:	Really?
Damien:	Yeah ...
Eva:	... So what kind of things would happen because of your temper?
Damien:	Fight ...

Often this difficulty with anger management resulted in a young person 'losing it' and causing damage to others and to property, sometimes almost unconsciously.

Anthony: I'm violent, I don't like to do, something just clicks, makes me go wild.

Eva: You, you've been wild and at the same time, you feel like you don't want to be wild?

Anthony: Yeah, like someone else is living inside me.

Tuscar: ... It's like when you're shouting, and it's something here anyway [points to chest]. It's something go up in your chest and that, just go mad, and that. Then, like, when you calm down and that, people say, 'Oh you've wrecked the place', and you just don't believe 'em and that.

These quotes illuminate the second concern in relation to perceptions of behaviour: the extent to which these young people feel they have control over their own actions. Clearly the interviewees above feel that their behaviour is outside of their own control. In this way, some of the interviewees identify their own temperament as a factor contributing to disruptive behaviour in school. Some interviewees even report that they take part in certain activities because they are fun or even irresistible.

Eva: Do you think it would be possible to just, you know, get on and do your work?

Sandra: Not really no, with other kids messing around, I can't help messing around with 'em, like messing around like, try messing around with 'em back.

Eva: ...would it have been possible for you not to mess about?

Carl: ... No.

Eva: I wonder why that is?

Carl: I dunno, cause like with your mates and that you get into messing about, like ...

Eva: It was just like a habit that you just kind of .....What do you think would have happened if you had gone into class and tried not to mess about?

Carl: ... I don't know ... but um, that won't happen though because the rest of the kids would be messing about.

Both these comments involve interactions with peers in school. The interviewees often report that their peers are implicated in disruptive behaviour. Carl's comment highlights the issue of the classroom environment and its influence on individuals' behaviour. Five of the young people speak of having difficulty managing their behaviour when they are with a large group of peers in a classroom. This is particularly true when they perceive their peers to be misbehaving and contributing to general classroom disruption.

Nahim: Before like, everyone is shouting their heads off, and talking, and girls laughing about something else.

Eva: Right.

Nahim: And somebody wrestling on the other side of the class.

Eva: Right.

Nahim: And then everybody messing around, teacher never used to do anything.

Eva: Right.

Nahim: So, you might as well mess around. You won't be able to do any work, 'cause you can't even think properly with all that noise going on.

Over one-third of the interviewees attributed at least some of their behaviour to their friends' influence. Some talked about getting into 'the wrong crowd' or living in 'bad areas'. They talked about taking part in disruptive activities with, and often under the influence of, friends. Some felt that they were required to engage in disruptive behaviour to maintain their standing within a particular friendship group.

Danni: ... It all started when I went to [secondary school], I got in with a bad crowd really.

Wayne: I just told her [mother] the truth – it wasn't my fault. I was following all my friends. They was my big friends, and I just followed 'em. I didn't know where I was going really and I didn't want to walk home at night on my own. So I just followed 'em.

Michelle: Nah, it was, uh, at school it was more like trying to be big like, in front of the other kids. Like say, 'Ah, look. I can do this,' and that.

Eva: Right. And what kind of things would you try and do?

Michelle: Like trying to impress other people like by shouting and
             mouthing off at the teachers and that.

In some instances, peers provoked the disruptive behaviour of interviewees.

Sarah: ...yeah, other pupils, like, my friends like. But they
             knew that, if like I done something, if they said something to
             me, I'd start. And then like the teachers say something, and
             they used to like me shouting at the teachers, so, they just
             used to enjoy it.

Anthony: And what made me kick the table over, was this, some kid,
             dealing drugs in the school.
Eva: Right.
Anthony: And he got caught, he said he got them off me, and it was
             nothing to do with me, so I booted and threw things and just
             went actually mad like.

As we will see in Chapter Four, teachers are also cited as a source of provocation of disruptive behaviour. Relations with teachers and relations
with peers are discussed in detail in the next two chapters. Of relevance
here is the young people's perceptions of their own behaviour and how
they attribute their behaviour to internal or external factors. All the
comments that attribute disruptive behaviour to peers give a sense that
many of the interviewees perceive themselves to be incapable of controlling their behaviour in the face of peer pressure or provocation. But a
few of the interviewees do seem to feel as if they control or 'own' their
behaviour.

Eva: ...is there any way that could have been different, so that you
             didn't end up getting in trouble?
Kirsty: I could have stopped myself really, but I didn't want to. I
             wanted to like, me and school was a let down, I didn't care
             about an education at all.
Eva: Right.
Kirsty: So I was, liked to play up, I wish I never, 'cause I miss my
             friends. But I couldn't stand that school, so I'm not getting on.

Michael: Some days I'd be on my good, kind one, to do good, kind
             things. Some days like, teachers just got my back up, and
             some days half of it's my fault, and half of it's the teachers
             fault...

Also included in this group are some of the interviewees mentioned earlier who feel they make conscious choices to take part in disruptive activities because they are 'fun'.

Danni: We thought it was quite funny by going round hitting all the fire alarms.

Joshua: And they were telling me that I shouldn't mix with them people. But I found them interesting I suppose, funny and everything.

Eva: Interesting and funny?

Joshua: Yeah, like they used to have a laugh and they just made me laugh, doing funny things ... they used to get in trouble and they used to find it funny. And I just started hanging about with them, used to go out with them sometimes after school I didn't get in trouble out of school. Just I suppose I found It funny so I started hanging about with them.

The majority of interviewees, however, seem to feel that at least some of their behaviour is outside of their control. This is either because they feel unable to resist the pressure of peers to behave in certain ways or because they feel unable to control their emotional responses to situations. Ownership over behaviour is not characterised by clear racial or gender differences. Most interviewees seem to feel that their immediate situation, personal characteristics or both result in some of their behaviour being out of their control.

Conclusion

Explaining behaviour is a complex task. The factors contributing to a disruptive incident include the personal characteristics of the student involved, the specific set of circumstances leading up to an incident, and the actions and responses of others involved in the situation. Subsequent chapters discuss the interviewees' accounts of situational factors and the role of other actors in shaping their experiences of school. By offering insight into the interviewees' views of their permanent exclusion and how they understand their own behaviour, this chapter has provided a foundation for what follows. Young people's perceptions of themselves and their behaviour will surely impact on the perceptions of their interactions with others and it is these interactions that are discussed next. In addition to laying the foundation from which to read the rest of the book, the young people's views on their behaviour provide us with information that is valuable for our practice.

We see significant differences in the interviewees' accounts of their experiences and understandings of their role in these experiences. These different understandings have implications for intervention. Those young people who described themselves as 'easy to wind up' or 'short-tempered' saw their disruptive behaviour as a direct expression of key aspects of their personalities. Other interviewees seemed to view their disruptive behaviour as something they did that was not necessarily an expression of who they are. They seem to be saying 'I am a good person even if I've done bad things'. For the first group of young people, behaviour and identity are inextricably linked, so intervention aiming to change behaviour would probably need to address the question of identity. A key task would be to help the individual re-conceptualise him or herself as being something other than 'easy to wind up' or 'bad tempered'. For the second group, who sees some of their behaviour as separate from their identity (it is the behaviour that is problematic) intervention might be distinctively different. Intervention with these students would be much more focused on behaviour itself, exploring the conditions under which such problematic behaviour occurs and how these conditions can be altered to bring about change.

4

Relationships with Teachers

Of all the topics the students discussed during interviews, relationships with teachers dominated – taking up the most interview time, eliciting the greatest detail and the strongest emotions. The aim of this chapter is to represent the views of the young people about their relationships with teachers, and then to 'use' these accounts to paint a picture of how the teacher-student relationship could be different. There are important messages here for teachers, particularly those who work with disaffected young people. The interviewees' accounts provide the opportunity to enter into the young person's perspective. This perspective is both insightful and immediately applicable to teachers' practice.

When considering the perspectives of young people who have been permanently excluded from school, it would be easy to assume that their described relations with teachers would be wholly antagonistic and negative. Although many of the young people interviewed in this study do describe difficult relationships with teachers, this experience was not universal. Further, most of the young people who described antagonistic relations with some teachers also described more positive interactions with others. Their views are often expressed with emotion, and also with thoughtfulness, insight and reflection. Far from being exceptional, this appears to be the norm in research with young people. Researchers have found young people perceptive (Whyte and Brockington, 1983), willing and seemingly uninhibited (Blatchford, 1996) and capable of providing invaluable information and insights (Bealing, 1990). And importantly, all these researchers and others have found the consistency of student response provides powerful messages for the education system.

The mass of data relating to the interviewees' perceptions of their relationships with teachers is presented in four sections. The first represents the interviewees' views on teacher qualities that they like and dislike. It is primarily descriptive and provides an insight into the aspects of the teachers' role that are most significant for these young people and that serve either to foster or hinder the development of positive relations. The next section focuses on a particular set of interactions: disciplinary practice. Unsurprisingly, discipline in schools is a particularly significant topic for the excluded students in this study. In this section we begin to access the reasoning employed by the interviewees to judge teacher actions as either appropriate or inappropriate. Justice emerges as an important theme and this theme is explored in the third section, which focuses on the ways in which the interviewees define and understand this concept. The fourth section considers how the interviewees understand the social structure within which their relationships with teachers are formed and operate. Their essential understanding is that this system is hierarchical and serves to disadvantage low-status students such as themselves.

The final section of the chapter seeks to integrate the findings of all four sections. The perceptions of the interviewees are integrated and used to develop an ideal model of teacher-student relations. This model reconsiders power relations in order to create a set of interactions that recognises the students' non-child status while, at the same time, highlighting teacher-specific responsibilities such as duty of care. Before discussing the interviewees' accounts of their relationships with teachers, an attempt is made to define the spectrum of views from which these accounts are derived. Despite the overall significance of relationships with teachers, there are some differences in the interviewees' perspectives and the dimensions and extent of these differences are explored to help to provide a context from which to read and understand their subsequent comments.

I recognise that the data concerning the teacher-student relationship presents the views of only one of the parties involved in that relationship. The views of the teachers have not been sought. Although the teachers' accounts would provide further insight into this key relationship, gaining their perceptions was beyond the scope of this study. The focus here has been to gain an in-depth understanding of the perspectives and ex-periences of a broad range (and relatively large number) of excluded students.

Defining the spectrum

Understanding the consistency and variance in the perspectives of the interviewees on their relationships with teachers is important. Their views can be considered along a spectrum of which their are two defin-ing dimensions. The first is concern with the nature of the relationship, ranging from positive to antagonistic. In this study there are two young people who each stands alone in their views, and each defines one end of the spectrum: Leon and Tonya.

Leon's difficulties in school and eventual exclusion were the result of his involvement in aggressive and often criminal activity with groups of young men in and outside school. He felt that the teachers in his school were supportive of him and made every effort to keep him at the school.

> Leon: Yeah, it was OK, like they respected me, I respected them. Like I done the teachers favours and they done favours back. It was like that.
>
> Eva: Oh yeah? What kind of favours can teachers do for you?
>
> Leon: It depends. Like if I was in trouble they used to only give me a warning. They'd never used to like tell me off or go to my parents or anything...Whenever I had problems I used to go to them and talk about it. That's the trust we had between each other.

Leon describes the teachers at school and at the Centre in positive terms. He seems to view them as allies.

Tonya, who had been excluded only six months before the interview, felt strongly antagonistic towards the teachers at her excluding school. She held them responsible for much of her behaviour which was deemed problematic at the school.

> Tonya: Yeah, I just don't, I can't really communicate with teachers... It's like, after a while I just cut them off, 'cause I don't ... you know, the teachers they don't know nothing there about you... that's what I think of them. I don't like teachers, I would never be a teacher, I'd never ... you know, talk to a teacher

> because at the end of the day look what they've done to me.
> I'm in this Centre I'm supposed to be at... school doing my
> GCSEs, do you get me? But I'm not, 'cause of them ... and
> the way they went on towards me.

Tonya did describe positive relationships with some of the teachers at the Centre and one teacher at school but her constructs for teachers as a collective group were strongly negative.

Very few of the sample described either wholly positive or wholly antagonistic relations with teachers. Most fell somewhere along the spectrum defined by Leon and Tonya. Several described having generally harmonious relations with most of the teaching staff but significant antagonistic relations between themselves and one or two teachers. Others described a generally hostile environment in which they had extremely positive relationships with one or a few teachers. Some interviewees described variable relations with all their teachers and a handful seemed ambivalent about their interactions with teachers.

The second dimension which defines the spectrum of interviewees' views on teachers is the powerful impact on their school experience of their relationships with teachers. Also important to them were their relationships with peers, and factors in their lives outside school such as their home life (see Phelan *et al.*, 1993 for discussion of Students' Multiple Worlds). The significance of their relations with teachers to their experience of school varied. Some saw it as *the* central feature of their school experience, others described it as one of several salient features of the experience, while a smaller number seemed to view the teachers as peripheral to their experience of school. This could often be determined by examining when and in what way the topic of 'teachers' arose in the interview. Although the interviews differed enormously, each began in the same way, with a question to the young person about which school they had last attended and what they thought of it. Often their response would highlight an issue or issues of particular importance to the individual that would then shape the rest of the interview. Consider the following four responses to the question 'What was your last school like?':

> Joshua: It was all right, I enjoyed it there, but I had problems with the teachers and stuff, but I enjoyed it there with my friends and all that.

Yvonne: It was crap, right. One, I reckon the only good thing about it was like, we had good work and that. What we did, we actually learnt something. And my friends. But teachers, weren't good.

Though one student describes school positively and the other negatively, they offer similar summaries of their individual experiences. Both enjoyed relationships with their peers and felt they were interested in learning. These two both identified their relationships and interactions with teachers as the area of difficulty at school. These relations were the most significant feature of their experience of school and the central focus of their accounts of it. Other interviewees identify different aspects of the school experience as important.

Sam: It was all right but, people just wanted to mess me around in there, so, to get me to fight and all that.

Sam highlights another key feature of the experience of school: relationships with peers. Conflict with other students was a prominent feature of Sam's experience of school. Although he regarded interactions and relationships with teachers as also significant, he did not necessarily see them as the most central feature of his experience, as Yvonne and Joshua did.

Tim: It was all right.
Eva: Yeah?
Tim: Yeah.
Eva: Can you remember the kinds of things you liked about it?
Tim: Don't know. [pause] Just messing about and that.

Tim's comment seems much less emotionally charged than those of his colleagues. Indeed, one senses a certain indifference in his response. Tim had not attended mainstream school for several years and his enduring memories were of time spent socialising with friends. He also spoke of significant aspects of life outside school, such as moving house on a number of occasions, and his relationship with his girlfriend. Relationships with teachers seemed to play a peripheral role in his experience of school. For students like Tim, relationships with peers and other factors in their lifes were presented as being more important than relationships with teachers. The impact of relationships with peers inside and outside school will be discussed in detail in the next two chapters.

Through an examination of the interview content and tone of response, the interviewees can be loosely categorised into three groups, according to their feelings about the importance of relationships with the teachers in their schools. Individuals are put into particular categories in light of my subjective assessment of their comments. Clearly it is difficult to quantify what people consider significant. The subjective classification does, however, provide some information about the extent to which the findings discussed in the paper reflect the experiences of the entire sample. The three groupings are those young people for whom inter-actions with teachers was central to their school experience (13), those who identified relationships with teachers as one of several salient features of their experience (12) and those for whom teachers seemed to play a peripheral role (8). In the latter group, inter-relations with teachers are often overshadowed by relationships with peers or circum-stances outside the school environment. Every effort has been made to represent the perspectives of the entire sample. It is possible that the views of the eight young people for whom teachers played a peripheral role will be somewhat under-represented as they made fewer comments about teachers than other interviewees.

Teacher qualities

In 1990 Woods reviewed much of the research done in the 1980s which commented on young people's perceptions of their teachers. He sum-marised the students' criteria for what constituted a 'good teacher', which included being human, being able to teach, having the ability to make students work and to maintain control. It was also important that teachers treat students with respect in order to earn respect in return. Finally, frequent mention was made of the importance of being able to talk to teachers (p.17-18). Ten years later, many of the themes are echoed as young people discuss the qualities of teachers they dislike as well as those they appreciate. Comments about the undesirable qualities of teachers were initially easier to elicit although, by the end of the data collection phase, examples of teachers' positive attributes were also abundant. As accounts of teachers' less desirable qualities were of greater salience to the interviewees as a whole, we will begin with these.

Undesirable teacher qualities

The qualities disliked by the interviewees fell into two groups. The first had to do with interpersonal relations between teachers and students, which they felt very personally. The second related to the more structural features of school life, such as the administration of school rules and concerns about lessons. We will begin with the first group, as comments about personal interactions were much more common than comments related to the structural features of school. Of all the interpersonal qualities of teachers that the young people found difficult, the most consistent and commonly cited grievance was that teachers did not listen to them. The charge of 'not listening' applied to a variety of situations.

> Danni: When I went to talk to 'em, like if I got into trouble, they wouldn't hear my side of the story. They'd take other people's side of the story, but they just wouldn't listen.

> Shelly: ...when you used to get SSR'd [Senior Staff Removal], you used to like have to be sent out for the lesson, like, and then go back at the end of the day to discuss it and that. But when you used to go back, like, all the teachers used to stick together. Like, when you tried to tell them what happened and that, the other teachers'd say 'Oh no, it didn't happen like that' and you'd get like more angry.

> Neil: They just wouldn't listen to you. Like, say you asked for help, they just wouldn't listen to you and just, I don't know....

> Sarah: ... [peers] just used to like, mess about with me and that used to get me really annoyed, and then I'd get into trouble, and then, when I'd tell the teacher that I was annoyed, they wouldn't listen to me, and tell me to shut up and sit down. And that's when I started arguing with the teachers.

There seem to be two bases upon which teachers' 'not listening' is deemed inappropriate. The first is a sense, on the part of students, that their point of view is not valued enough to be heard. The students perceive certain teachers as not valuing their views, either in their own right or when in direct competition with the views of other teachers. Undervaluing students' points of view in this way often leads young people to feel they have been treated unfairly, as in the following example.

Charles: ... so he said if I use it again then I'll be in trouble. And somebody else has gone 'BLOODY', and he's gone, 'right, get out now', and I goes 'that weren't me', and he wouldn't take it. So, they never listened, they just assumed that it's the naughtiest person in the class, which was me.

The comments of Neil and Sarah imply that teachers' 'not listening' is inappropriate also because such behaviour contradicts aspects of the teachers' professional role in facilitating learning, as highlighted by Neil, or in meeting young people's social and emotional needs, as noted by Sarah. Crozier and Antiss (1995) made the same point in their study of girls' perceptions of disruption: 'The girls were emphatic about the power of words to hurt and claimed that teachers did not take the problem seriously or do anything about it' (p.42). Either teachers do not recognise the significance to students of these interactions or there is an inconsistency between teachers' perceptions of their role *vis-á-vis* student relations and students' perceptions of the teachers' role. Clearly these students feel that it is the teachers' responsibility to intervene in and help 'sort out' student conflict.

Closely related to not feeling listened to, and almost as frequently reported, is the feeling that teachers exaggerated or even lied about students' behaviour. This is often related to reports which come to the young people's attention during or after their exclusion.

Joshua: Yeah because there were two sheets of paper with little writing. I was thinking I ain't done all that I don't remember. Some things, there were things on there that I never done before that I've never done in my whole life. There was one thing it says I forged a twenty pound note. I've never had one in my life, I don't know where it come from, I tried to tell the teacher that [I] ain't done many things on there, but [—] 'If you never done it then how comes it's on here?'. I would have known if I forged a twenty pound note.

Nahim: Um, they would have expelled me anyway, the head master wouldn't have, 'cause most of the things that they used to say about me wasn't true.

Eva: Right.

Nahim: Like, they was true, but they used to go and exaggerate, add more things on.

Eva:	Oh okay, do you have any examples of that?
Nahim:	Like, before when I used to wag it sometimes, they used to say, oh he wags it, and he messes around outside. And sometimes police used to walk past, and used to swear at the police. Like, when they walking up the streets they bully other kids, and they do this, and they do that.
Eva:	Mm mm.
Nahim:	And they drink.
Eva:	Right.
Nahim:	And they mess around a lot. The drinking part was true but the other part weren't true. We used to swear at the police sometimes.

It is difficult to determine the extent to which particular allegations are based on fact, and this research does not try to do so. What is clear is that a discrepancy exists between students' perceptions of their behaviour and teachers' accounts. What is also clear is that for many young people such discrepancies become obvious only when it is too late for anything constructive to be done about them. Another resonant feature of these comments is a sense of helplessness: the individual versus a larger, more powerful institution. The students' perceived helplessness and their belief that they are not liked are almost certainly realistic. The enduring message for many students is that they are alone and outside the system.

A large number of negative experiences can be loosely categorised as antagonistic behaviour by teachers: ignoring students, telling them to shut up, shouting, responding sarcastically, putting them down and calling them names. Collectively, such forms of behaviour are those most commonly mentioned by young people. The following examples illustrate various ways in which the students felt the teachers' behaviour to be antagonistic.

Yvonne:	There was no reason. Just things like that, what she was doing. I'd talk to her, like, she asked a question, I'd put my hand up to answer it, and she'd like, say you're me, she'd look round, and say, 'Anybody know the answer?' And like she hasn't seen me.
Joshua:	The teachers tells me to shut up. And I'd just start answering her back and being cheeky.

Eva:	Mmm and what does that feel like to be told to shut up?
Joshua:	I don't like being told to shut up by no one so I just get angry...

Tuscar:	... Couple of 'em was okay, but it was always just like. Just do your 'ead in, so.
Eva:	And how, for you, what would the teachers do, to do your head in?
Tuscar:	Just shout at me all the time.

Eva:	So the teachers are sarcastic?
Sarah:	Yeah.
Eva:	Can you tell me a little bit more about, about that?
Sarah:	Um... if I say something to you, say, like you'd just answer me in like, a funny way, and just used to annoy me. Didn't like it.

Charles:	...and he used to cuss us. He used to call us thick, he used to say we need a psychologist and everything.

Kirsty:	And like he's 'Oh you've got to do this', 'Sir I haven't got the sheet', 'Well get up there and get one then, you stupid cow'. All this.

Students commonly cite public humiliation, especially being shouted at, as one of the most negative teacher-student interactions. Such antagonistic teacher behaviour reminds us of the impact that teachers' words have on their students and particularly their sense of self-worth. The teachers' behaviour outlined above conveyed a message to students that they were not valued.

One type of antagonistic behaviour which deserves separate attention is behaviour which is racist. Six interviewees, five of them from ethnic minority groups, reported incidents of racism from teachers. Given that the total number of ethnic minority interviewees was fifteen, this constitutes a significant minority. Three mentioned teacher comments which were racist either in terminology or inference.

Nahim:	...And he used to talk to the black kids, and he used to say to them that, hang around with your own kind. Black people should hang around with black people. And Pakis should hang around with Pakis.
Eva:	Really?
Nahim:	He said: Pakis. He should have said Asians but he said Pakis...

The other three raised the issue of differential treatment based on race.

Damien:	And they was going to school the first day, I mean the desks were all in a row.
Eva:	Right.
Damien:	I just sat down and then he goes, 'You, come here'. And he's got the four black people sat in the front.
Eva:	Mm mm.
Damien:	And at the end of that day, the four people who got detained were the four people in the front row.

The topic of racism in schools was not explicitly part of the interview structure but was raised by the young people as a significant feature of their school experience. Perhaps if my questions had been more explicit, more such incidents would have been reported. Three of the young people who reported racist incidents are African-Caribbean, one is of mixed parentage, one Asian and one White-European. The complex and subtle nature of racism in schools has been discussed by, *inter alia*, Wright *et al.* (1998), Sewell (1997), Mac an Ghaill (1996), Gillborn and Gipps (1996). We have seen that teachers' behaviour towards students sends implicit messages to the students about their value in the class-room. Racist teacher behaviour, actual or perceived, will unquestionably have a negative impact on young people's sense of self and self-value.

The effect of these tacit messages on young people's esteem should not be underestimated. For many of the interviewees, poor relationships and negative interactions with teachers led them to feel unwanted in school. Several describe being 'disliked' or 'hated':

Anthony:	Mm. All the teachers just slagged me. I heard 'em, I heard 'em in the, um, staff room, and other people told me as well, you know. And I've heard 'em in the, when I got sent out my lessons, 'That Anthony's just a naughty piece of work, nasty piece of work', and all this. I'm not liked.
Eva:	Really. How did you get on with the teachers?
Nathan:	Didn't like them. And they didn't like me.
Eva:	Yeah
Nathan	A few of them did but, not many did.
Yvonne:	D'you know when you can tell people don't like you? And if it weren't their job to teach me, they wouldn't like me.

The teacher qualities mentioned thus far refer to personalised interactions between teachers and students. The next comments relate to
teachers in their role within the institution of school, including teaching
and also taking responsibility for upholding standards of behaviour.
How the rules were administered was often a contentious issue for the
young people in this study.

Jon:	Something like, if he catches you with your trainers on, he takes your trainers off you. Or with jewellery, he takes it off you. He makes you come down and get it. And like he don't give you no warnings or anything, or if you haven't got a pencil with you, you got a detention, and things like that.
Dana:	Yeah, I wore like, shoes like this [trainers] but in black and they weren't acceptable. But, like, it was all right for the other girls to wear six-inch platform shoes.
Eva:	Really.
Dana:	But, like, they could easily break their ankle and I'm in the most comfortable shoes.

Several of the young people commented on the lack of effort some
teachers put into lessons.

Nahim:	Like, you know when you're in a lesson, the teachers gonna be sitting there, and he's gonna write a couple of things on the board, and sit there and he's just gonna read the paper and you're gonna be just talking to your friends all the way through the lesson.
Eva:	Right.
Nahim:	Even in a double lesson, teacher never used to talk, or anything. Do the register and that's it. When the head master used to come to the classroom, then he used to get up and start reading a book or something, otherwise if he didn't he'd be sitting down all the lesson.
Nathan:	No, I had to change lessons but the other lesson I was doing the teacher was never there anyway.
Eva:	Really? And then what would you do?
Nathan:	... I built a park five times [given the assignment: Design a safe park for children]. He used to come in every lesson and say 'Carry on with your park' then he'd go away and we didn't have a park. We smashed it up every lesson.

These comments reflect the students' perception of their teachers as undervaluing them but also indicate that the students believe learning to be a valuable activity. The teacher's failure to facilitate learning is a large part of what is being criticised. It is well documented that the vast majority of young people in school wish to learn and succeed in school (Rudduck *et al.*, 1996; de Pear and Garner, 1996; Woods, 1990; Lloyd-Smith, 1984). Woods (1990) observes that, 'Even the apparently most anarchic pupils may want to work' (p.21). So it is not surprising that the students see teachers' failure to provide adequate learning opportunities as problematic. Also problematic is teachers' unwillingness to provide what students perceive as the help that they need to succeed in completing work.

Tuscar:	Like when they don't hear what the teacher says, and that, and she won't repeat it, so they start messing around and that, and then just shouts at 'em then.
Eva:	Right.
Tuscar:	Like, if she repeated like what she said in the first place, then I would do the work.
Michael:	Well, when I go up and talk to her, go, 'Can you explain this', and that, she'll go, 'Explain what? You've been doing it all, like, all term. This is what you've been taught'. And I don't understand what I'm doing ...
Shelly:	Well, uh, with...when I was there...when I was like having geography and that, like I didn't like the teacher and the lesson and that 'cause he used to just give you work and say 'Get on with it'. He didn't used to explain and that. And I didn't know what to do and that and he used to just start shouting and, like, saying, 'Get on with your work', and that and I just started, like, answering back and things like that.

To summarise, the interviewees disliked teachers they perceived to be unable or unwilling to meet their needs, including teachers who engaged in what they saw as antagonistic behaviour towards them. The needs that young people felt teachers should meet were both academic and pastoral. This included enabling students to learn and succeed in their school work as well as intervening in their non-academic lives so as to manage conflicts effectively between students and teachers, and among student peers.

Desirable teacher qualities

Existing research tells us quite a bit about the teacher qualities that students appreciate, for example, taking time to talk with and listen to students (Nieto, 1994; Cooper, 1992; Woods, 1990). Students also want teachers to understand and relate to their students (Howe, 1995; SooHoo, 1993; Gannaway, 1976) and to have a friendly approach and sense of humour, which students consider important in establishing and fostering relationships (Chaplain, 1996; Garner, 1995; Gannaway, 1976). The ability of teachers to establish positive relationships is of the utmost importance to the interviewees in this study. The qualities that students liked and appreciated about teachers related to their perceptions of teachers' responsibilities as both educators and pastoral carers. Interviewees appreciated teachers who would talk to and listen to them, who could 'have a laugh', and who openly showed care and concern for them. There follow some interviewees' descriptions of teachers and teacher-qualities they liked. The first three are about teachers at mainstream school and the last two about teaching staff in the Centres.

Eva:	So what was good about Mr Knight?
Yaz:	I just used to get on with him, if I had any problems, then I'd tell him.
Eva:	Right.
Yaz:	...and if I used to walk past him in the school...he'd stop me, 'Where you going, what you up to now?' And just to make sure that I weren't doing nothing wrong.
Eva:	Right.
Yaz:	He was a fun teacher and some days if I was really ill, and I didn't wanna go home, I just wanted to stay in school for a bit, he'd say, 'Well go and sit in my office then'...

Eva:	...What was it about her that you were able to get on with her?
Anthony:	I dunno, she just, she was always interested in listening to me.

Eva:	What kind of things would a teacher do and you would think 'Oh that teacher is alright?
Jade:	... What kind of things?
Eva:	Yeah, like what would they be like?
Jade:	... After school they'd take me to the weight gym, that was all right.
Eva:	Oh wow.

Jade:	I can... go in the gym and play basketball and that.
Lorraine:	It's just, you get all the attention that you need. [in the BSS Centre]
Eva:	Mm mm.
Lorraine:	And you can talk to the teachers anytime. I mean, when you're in the lesson or you know, break time or whatever. It's just, they're just, down to earth, really down to earth. They're not stuck up or anything, and thinking, 'Oh God, here she comes again'...
Nathan:	You know when two adults are talking about something....
Eva:	Yeah.
Nathan:	Or when you're talking with your mate and you're talking about stuff that you believe in and stuff? You can with the teachers here as well.

These quotations sum up the points made by the sample as a whole. In contrast to the teacher behaviours that students disliked, which left them feeling undervalued, the students welcomed the active efforts teachers made to establish relationships with students. These teachers were seen to go out of their way at times to ensure that young people were given the attention they needed. The interviewees respond most positively to the teachers they perceived as abandoning a distant teacher-student relationship model in favour of a certain type of friendship model. This fulfils the needs students have for teachers to take on a pastoral role in their interactions with them and to demonstrate care and concern for them.

Another quality valued in teachers is their ability to educate – that is, to impart skills and knowledge to their students. Although there was some variability in the interviewees' desire to learn, the ability to teach subject knowledge was nevertheless important to many of the young people. They regard part of the ability to teach as the willingness to give students the attention and help they need in order to learn.

| Nahim: | She was like, she used to be real good at drawing, and she used to give you lots of good tips. She used to always talk to you, never used to shout. And she never used to shout at the class and they never used to talk. |
| Eva: | Really. |

Nahim:	They used to just get on with the work. 'Cause like, she used to give us things to do, and you know like she, uh, you're happy that you're doing it.
Eva:	And so the teachers that you did like, what were the things... what were they like?
Shelly:	Um, well the teachers that I liked, they used to be all right and that. They used to, like, show me what to do with the work and they used to, like, talk to me like how I'd like to be talked to and things like that.

It is well documented in the literature that students appreciate teachers who make an effort to teach in an interesting and effective way (Wallace, 1996, Nieto, 1994, Woods, 1990). This view is expressed by students in mainstream school and those in alternative provision.

The ability to establish relationships and enjoy interactions with young people and at the same time enable the young people to learn was, on the whole, particularly valued, but this did not hold true for all the interviewees. A handful explained that they liked teachers who let them 'get away' with things.

Yaz:	And that's why I liked History 'cause she just used to let us carry on, she'd tell us what to do, and then carry on ...

Many of the young people, however, seemed to most appreciate teachers who could bridge the gap between 'friendship' and discipline by incorporating the two into lessons.

Michael:	...My English teacher is another one. He's got good hearing.
Eva:	Oh yeah.
Michael:	Got good hearing. If you sit at the back of the room and start talking, 'Psst, psst, psst', and you can hardly hear yourself, and he will look up and go, 'Stop talking you two'. Sometimes he'd have a laugh with you, but when it comes to being serious, he is serious. And we're serious back.
Manny:	It was all right, Miss and it was quite easy to do as well, Miss and the teacher was good teacher as well, Miss. He didn't mind you talking, and as long as you get on with your work, Miss.

By examining the teacher qualities which the young people found desirable, a profile of a good teacher emerges. For the students interviewed, a good teacher was primarily one who was able to establish meaningful relationships with students and was able to teach.

We have seen that most young people express a desire to learn and succeed. The teacher qualities that the interviewees like and dislike are summarised in the table below. It comes as no surprise that the interviewees liked best those teachers who made them feel valued and worthwhile as individuals, and also as students capable of learning.

Discipline and behaviour

Another key issue for the young people is discipline. All the interviewees had experienced disciplinary action at school – the universal experience was of being the person on the receiving end of disciplinary action. The group's perspective on the nature and efficacy of various forms of discipline are insightful and enlightening.

Interestingly, several of the interviewees commented that their teachers should have been stricter. Although a few, such as Yaz, said that they

Figure 4.1: Summary of Teacher Qualities Liked and Disliked

Disliked	Liked
not listening	talking to and listening to students
exaggerating/lying	having a laugh
ignoring	showing concern
telling to shut up	teaching well/being skilled
shouting	explaining/offering help
being sarcastic	keeping control of class
insulting	
racially discriminating	
authoritarian administration of rules	
poor teaching	
not helping	

liked teachers who let them do what they liked, many of the interviewees saw a need for their teachers to maintain discipline. They felt that teachers should take responsibility for controlling the behaviour of the students.

> Eva: Oh yeah, what was that like as a school?
>
> Carl: It was okay but, em, there was no restriction, could mess about in there...
>
> Eva: So what would be better about being strict?
>
> Carl: ... Um ... like show you a bit more discipline and everything.
>
> Sarah: Yeah, I dunno why. But like, I think it's, I dunno, I think I needed to have more strict teachers. Like, if I'd have had, like, stricter teachers teaching, then I probably would have got on better at the school. 'Cause, like, I behaved for them. But like, teachers who like, can't control ya, I had quite a few of them. And um, I just didn't get on.

The call for more vigilant disciplinary action is not unique to this study. Bealing (1990) asked a group of students with records of truanting from school what could be done about truancy. Their suggestions included taking registers at every lesson, cross-checking with tutors, spot-checking the toilets for students absent from lessons, and phoning the students' homes at the earliest sign of trouble (p.29). Although the expressed need for greater disciplinary action partly reflects the young people's reluctance to assume responsibility for their own or their peers' behaviour, it also reflects their understanding of the role of teachers. Clearly the young people feel that teachers are responsible for the monitoring and ultimate control of student behaviour (or certainly misbehaviour).

In the last section we saw that students value friendly personal relationships with teachers, but these are not without precise limitations. The parameters which define the nature of teacher-student friendships are based on the teachers' roles within the institution, one perceived aspect of which is to maintain a certain standard of behaviour. At times the students' wishes for teachers to establish less formal relationships seems to conflict with their belief that teachers should regulate certain behaviour.

Nahim: ...Mr Holder he was all right, but only one thing about him was, he never used to grass off everybody.

Eva: Right, so is that good or...?

Nahim: I thought it was good at first, but then I thought in my head, I thought if he, he grasses up me, that I've been wagging it and everything, then I won't do it again. But why doesn't he grass on me? Teachers are supposed to grass. That's what they get paid for, they get paid for teaching and if something's happening, they get paid to inform the parents as well, ain't it. So why ain't they doing it? I thought, nah, he's my good friend like so he's doing it not to get me into trouble.

Nahim's comment shows the confusion he experiences when a teacher he likes does not assume what Nahim feels is the responsibility of his role as a teacher.

So the young people seem to see maintaining discipline as an important aspect of the teachers' role. What then is the nature of the discipline they advocate? From previous sections it is clear that some forms of being 'strict' are definitely considered unacceptable, such as shouting or belittling students in the presence of peers. When the interviewees call for teachers to be stricter, they seem to describe a particular kind of disciplinary practice characterised by fair and appropriate sanctions for a misdemeanour.

Jon: Oh, I got suspended for being in a fight, yeah, I think that's fair.

Tuscar: And the PE teachers ... they just like shout if you done something wrong, don't they? But, the other ones just shout for the fun of it.

Eva: Oh really, wow. So what other kind of things that, you reckon, you know, deserve being shouted at?

Tuscar: ... Um, when I was in PE, I didn't really get shouted at, except when I was throwing the ball over the fence and that, on purpose. Like, things what, like, that you know you're doing wrong, just shout at you then.

Michael: ...'Cause you think of a good way, what it needs putting to. Say, like, if I kick somebody, do something in that area.

Eva: Right.

Michael:	Rounders, or if I kick something, do something, give me some kind of punishment to do with...not going out and kicking people again.
Eva:	Right.
Michael:	So that would mean stopping in at break and not going out for dinner.
Eva:	Right.
Michael:	If I've been in trouble in lessons, put me on report. If I don't come to school, then talk to me about it. Don't just come in and go, 'You haven't been in school, I'm putting you on report. Bye-bye'.

One part of fair discipline is the importance of ascertaining all sides of a story.

Eva:	... how do you think the teachers should be with students?
Gary:	Listen to both sides of the story and then put them together and then come to a conclusion. Like to both of ya because, like in that school I've just been expelled from, they always just sort of put it down to one person and goes, 'Ah, like, we'll chuck him out'. Just like that, 'cause they ain't really bothered, I don't think. It's just one more student to them.
Eva:	... what should they have done if there was a fight or something?
Jade:	They should have asked around what happened. I don't know, they just suspend me for a couple of days that's what they do, and they just give you a warning 'Can't fight in the school'.

The way discipline is applied is also important to the interviewees – both the tone in which disciplinary comments are made and the clear outline of the individual teacher's disciplinary procedure. In the following comments, the young people provide concrete examples of disciplinary interaction which they judge to be appropriate.

Kirsty:	Helped ya, not like shouting, shouting at ya, being more polite to ya, being there when you need to talk to 'em. Um, like, give you like a warning like, to get your earrings out like, 'don't wear 'em tomorrow'. But put it the right way, like, 'you shouldn't do this, you should do this'. Like, as time going on teachers like shouting out in the classroom... 'Get them

earrings out NOW, DO IT NOW, or your going home', and all this. I don't care, I thought, I wouldn't get my earrings out, so send me home.

Leon: Like, 'Do this, do that, don't do this'. They [good teachers] said that as well, but in a politer way. Like they explained. That sort.

Eva: Does that make a difference, explaining?

Leon: Mm-hmm it does. It makes a lot of difference. Saying in a friendly kind of way – it depends how you say it.

Not only was an appropriate response to misdemeanours and a 'friendlier' tone important, but the disciplinary action should serve an educational function. Kirsty has been quoted saying that teachers should frame their reprimands by saying 'You should do this, you shouldn't do this', revealing a view that discipline should serve not only to manage activity in the classroom but also to provide guidance on appropriate behaviour. The importance of the educational function of discipline is highlighted when students comment on forms of punishment that do not work. Suspension from school (fixed-term exclusion) is often described as an ineffective consequence.

Charles: ... When I got suspended, it was just like staying off school for a week. You just waited until after school, and then you go out. So it don't matter. We just stay in bed, as long as you want, and get up when you want, and everything, so... there ain't no point suspending people.

Lorraine: Yeah, they should have done, they should have sent me there before [a BSS Centre], and it's like, have a little bit of a break, instead of suspending me all the time.

Eva: Oh I see.

Lorraine: Because it doesn't do nothing, I'm just at home, and like, that's it. I'm just at home, and there was no teacher that I could talk to, 'cause normally there'd be a teacher in the school, or someone from the Bridge Centre who would come and talk to you, like 'em, what is it? Like a Social Worker or something like that.

Eva: Educational Social Worker, maybe?

Lorraine: Yeah, yeah someone like that. But they never done that, they just kept on suspending me. I'm not learning from that anyway, 'cause, it's just nothing really.

These students reject fixed-term exclusion as an effective sanction for misbehaviour on the grounds that it fails to provide any learning or guidance to them about their actions and interactions.

In addition to sharing their views about how disciplinary consequences could best be administered, the interviewees highlight quite another aspect of behavioural management: preventative intervention. For some, preventative intervention meant discipline at an early stage, without serious sanctions.

> Nahim: Next day go in late, they used to keep track of anybody that, missed out lots of days, they used to phone your house up and used to find out why you never come.
>
> Eva: Right.
>
> Nahim: Hillcrest, never went there for about two months, and they didn't have the phone number or anything, they wasn't organised. Cause everyone used to mess around, they used to say, 'What's the point?'
>
> Eva: So do you think they should have phoned home?
>
> Nahim: I wouldn't have got kicked out if they would have phoned home to my parents.

> Lorraine: ...like Mr Jennings [Centre teacher] yesterday, phone me mom, 'cause I never went to [a regular placement assisting in a primary school]. He phoned my mom, so he could see if there's anything wrong. Like is there any problems at home, that's what he asked my mom. And then he could see. In Marchant's Hall they didn't see, they didn't see nothing.
>
> Eva: And you, feel that, that what Mr Jennings did, is what teachers should do?
>
> Lorraine: Yeah, they should do that

In both these cases, the early link with home was seen as a central feature of preventative disciplinary action. These moments needed to be carefully chosen, however. As one young man pointed out, early discipline that is deemed unnecessary could create unforeseen problems for young people and their families.

> Richard: ...think we [Richard and his mother] used to argue about doing the washing up and stuff like that, ... like the teacher used to send out um silly reasons like, forget my pencil case or something like that, 'Richard forgot his pencil case for two

days'. Like, letters from the school used to really piss my mom off, cause there used to be a pile of 'em at home, like that, just silly reasons.

Other interviewees commented on preventative interventions that took place during school time. They noted the ability of some teachers to recognise potentially volatile situations and intervene before any serious disruption did take place.

Perry: ... say the mood I felt in before I go on the playground, I would have end up hitting someone, you know what I'm saying. So what I used to do, is, I used to go and see Mr Reid, he used to put me on the computers all dinner time like. Didn't have to – used to go out of his way. Open the computer cupboard, know what I mean, didn't have to do that, didn't have to come out of his lunch, come and open the computer cupboard and then come after his lunch and close it, but he knew man, he did it for me, you know what I'm saying?

Yaz: But Mr Knight would always be able to calm me down, and just say things what would calm me down, 'there's no point in doing that cause you know what Miss Dover's like, she won't let you straight in straight away', or, 'if you do that, then you've got this to...'. He just used to speak to me properly.

Richard: Like it was bad in year seven, and year eight got all right, in year nine was okay, 'cause I had, in year nine I used to just, I had this year tutor called Miss Dixon.
Eva: Mm mm.
Richard: She was saying, she always used to tell when I came in of a morning, and afternoon, she always used to tell if I was in a mood, and she used to sit down and listen. 'Sit over here and read a book' or something like that...

What are the skills attributed to the teachers in these situations? In each case the teacher is described as recognising the young person's state of volatility, suggesting that there are certain circumstances that can lead to a predictable pattern of interactions that can result in the student 'getting into trouble'. Given that the pattern is predictable, the skill required by the teacher (and praised by the student) is to recognise the pattern at the early stages and intervene appropriately. The intervention itself does not reflect what we often think of as disciplinary action. In two of the cases the students are offered alternative activities to divert them from potential conflict with peers. In the third case, the teacher speaks to the student in private, reminding her of the reality of the situation and the consequences of particular lines of action. Inherent in the young people's accounts is a sense that the teachers knew the young people personally and that they cared for them.

Clearly the young people feel that effective discipline is necessary in schools but what they deemed effective does not always reflect traditional notions of discipline. The ideal disciplinary practice advocated by the interviewees can be characterised as follows:

• Discipline should be preventative when possible.

• When prevention is not possible, punishment should be fair, appropriate to the misdemeanour, and delivered in a respectful manner.

• Discipline should serve to educate.

• Disciplinary action should be motivated by a concern for the well-being of students.

The notion of justice

Inherent in the young people's comments on discipline is the notion of justice – what is fair and what is not. Research into the views of disaffected students often cites injustice as a significant theme in the young people's discourse. Many young people who are excluded from school speak of the injustice of their exclusion (de Pear, 1997; Kinder *et al.*, 1997; Cohen and Hughes, 1994). Researchers into youth perspectives comment on the importance to students of teachers being fair and punishing justly (Rudduck *et al.*, 1996; Woods, 1990). Already in this chapter we have seen that certain teacher behaviours, such as not listening, evoke a sense of injustice.

The 'justice' of which the young people speak is both consistently defined across interviews and highly specific in its definition. For the young people interviewed, justice meant equality and equality was closely tied to parity of treatment and reciprocity of behaviour. When students were treated differently from their peers for what they saw as equivalent behaviour, they regarded this as unfair.

Neil: They just wouldn't listen to you. Like, say you asked for help, they just wouldn't listen to you and just, I don't know....just shout at you when you're hardly doing anything wrong and someone else is doing something more wrong.

Lorraine: That's it, you should just be treated equally. I mean, probably be a good child, right, and then they'll be a bad one. You know that a bad one's gonna be, like, told off and everything, be just treated badly. But I want to just be treated equally. Everyone should be just given a chance.

Charles: But then they would start crying. But if we started crying, and went to the teacher, they'd say, 'Shut up, being a baby,' But they didn't 'cause it's a girl.

Eva: So, do you feel that it was different treatment for boys and girls?

Charles: It was. 'Cause we weren't allowed to go to the toilet during lessons ... so, and they was allowed to sit by who they wanted, and we weren't because we'd mess about.

These young people were highly attuned to any teacher's differential treatment of students. They seemed quick to notice such treatment, particularly as they perceived themselves to be disadvantaged by it. When disciplinary action was seen as necessary, the interviewees felt that it must be administered evenly and consistently for all students. It was important for the same or similar offences to be met with the same response – only this was fair.

Leon: Well, I think it was okay [Centre response to a fight]. This one was fair, like, in a way. Because they expelled both of us.

Eva: Right.

Leon: And they brought us back on the same day and they told both of us the exact same thing. If we do it once more then that's it.

Tim: ... and the teacher grabbed me – I was on my final warning – and the teacher grabbed me and he said like 'Go up to my office now'. And I go 'No, you haven't done nothing when he [a peer] started earlier but now you're telling me to go to your office. I'm not going to go to your office'.

Joshua: ... because I got suspended twice and I got expelled and um, other people, this one kid Raj I used to hang about with, he got suspended seven times and he's still in school now. So I got suspended twice, I got expelled on the third time. I don't think that was fair, when other people are getting like something like seven, four, five chances.

Charles: And that was like me and Mark that got done for that, but he didn't get suspended and I did. She said 'You can't suspend him because he'll be on the streets', and they didn't want him on the streets cause his mum didn't care about him, or something. So they didn't suspend him.

Eva: What do you think of that?

Charles: It's not...they should've suspended him anyway, because you can't suspend one without the other.

The final quote in particular demonstrates a certain rigidity in the students' ideas about the 'fair' administration of disciplinary action. All the comments reveal that the equality which underlies the interviewees' sense of justice is characterised by identical treatment. The teachers' treatment of students is constantly under scrutiny and, to be deemed fair, they must be seen to behave consistently towards all students. As we have seen, this strict adherence to same-treatment was of prime importance in the allocation of reprimand.

The principle which governed students' behaviour towards teachers was apparently reciprocity. Incidentally, the students spent much less time scrutinising and discussing their own behaviour than that of teachers. In many cases, they perceived their behaviour to mirror the teacher's. Bad behaviour would be met with bad behaviour, while good or kind treatment would be likewise reciprocated.

Sam: No, if they don't wanna listen to me, I don't listen to them. Give it 'em back.

Leon: Yeah, it was OK, like they respected me, I respected them.

Kirsty: Our teachers [Centre], teachers are nice to me, so I'm nice to them, speak to ya kind.

It was interesting that the pervading view was that acts of kindness had always to begin with the teacher.

Eva: Sounds like a lot of what you're talking about is, is respect.

Tonya: Mm, that's all you need at the end of the day, they can respect you, obviously you can respect them.

...

Eva: Right, so does the respect need to come from them first?

Tonya: Yeah, you have to show a little respect.

Eva:...   I mean you said that for the, in the younger years it was just, treat you with respect, so then you treated them with respect. Do you think it, does it have to come from the teachers first, the respect?

Kirsty: ... Mm yes and no, like coming here didn't know what the teachers was like, we had a lesson and they treat me with respect, give them respect. In my old school I think I was waiting for, like, give me respect.

Thus the interviewees' moral evaluation of teacher-student interactions revolved around a particular notion of justice. The form of justice adhered to by the young people hinged on and was defined by parity of treatment and reciprocity of action. Scrutiny of behaviour as either just or unjust was applied almost exclusively to the action of teachers. Any behaviour by a teacher perceived contrary to these notions was deemed unfair and deeply resented.

Another theme runs through the interviewees' moral evaluations of teacher behaviour – the theme of care. As we saw earlier, the students advocate disciplinary action which is perceived to be both fair and *motivated by a concern for the well-being of students*. Several interviewees cited special treatment afforded them by a particular teacher, such as the use of computers at lunch-time, permission to sit in a tutor's office when feeling ill or being allowed to read a book instead of engaging in classroom activities. Never is this behaviour criticised on the grounds that it was not offered equally to all students. It seems that specific acts which place the interviewee in a position of relative privilege are exempt from judgement along the defined paradigm of justice. Rather, equality, parity and reciprocity become significant when the interviewees see themselves as disadvantaged relative to their peers. 'Justice' emerges as an issue when the young people see themselves as being treated differently *and more negatively* than their peers; that is, when their needs to be cared for are not met.

Often it is the young people's perception of teachers caring or not caring which determines whether or not a behaviour is considered just. As we have seen, the action of contacting parents for minor misdemeanours can be heralded as effective intervention or, alternatively, seen as a sort of harassment, depending on the perceived motivation for making this contact. Once again, students' moral evaluation of teacher behaviour is shaped by their perceptions of the role of teachers. Teachers are seen as both educators and carers; if they fail to meet the students' academic or pastoral needs, they are deemed unfair. Further, if teachers are seen to go beyond simply ignoring students and actively engage in behaviour which is seen as personally insulting and damaging to a young person's self-esteem, this too is viewed as breaching the young people's notion of what can be considered just.

Hierarchy as the social framework in school

All the interactions described thus far take place within the social system of school. Understanding the way in which young people comprehend this system helps us to contextualise their perceptions. It also helps us to gain insight into the nature of the system itself.

In school, the framework which underlies the young people's interpretation of events and interactions within that social system is the framework of hierarchy. Interactions are seen to take place between individuals who hold different positions in a hierarchy. Most clearly, the young people interviewed perceive themselves as occupying the lowest position in the hierarchy while teachers assume the highest. The interviewees identify a hierarchical imbalance in the teacher-student relationship and clearly identify that teachers possess an unequal and greater share of power.

Tuscar: Yeah, I got on with all of them [students]. Just that I don't like teachers, and it's like they think that they're higher than you. Like just 'cause they like try and teach me how to work and that, think like they higher than you, and things like that, so.

Tonya: ... You can't make a person talk to you like dirt and you're talking to them like they're Queen and King. And you know I couldn't do that.

Yvonne: ...And then he started, he started shouting at me, telling me that I'm wasting... And I just said 'Sir, why you shouting at me?' 'cause I mean he just start shouting, I says, 'There's no need to shout' and then he got even more angry', 'cause I told him there's no need to shout, and told me if I carried on, I'm going to have to go home. I says, 'But, why, I just told you not to shout at me. But [if] I turned round and started shouting at you first, right, you'd call me rude. So why is there any difference, it's just a age group. If you want respect off me, you've got to give it back'. And that really got him mad.

Joshua: Like I didn't used to start it, the teacher would tell me to shut up first and I would say something back to her like I would say, what are you telling me to shut up for Miss. Like I'm not no dog don't speak to me like that and tell her to be quiet. And then the teacher would just say shut up and get out the class and go wait. 'What have I done?' And it would just build up from there.

Some students, such as Tuscar and Yvonne, question the very basis upon which the hierarchy stands. The majority of interviewees, however, were more apt to take issue with *how* teachers managed their privileged position. This will be discussed in more detail later in this chapter.

There was also a sense, for many young people, that certain students were higher in the school hierarchy than themselves. Several of the interviewees felt that they and some of their peers held the lowest positions in the hierarchy, while other students enjoyed a preferential status in relation to the teachers.

Eva: I mean is there, did they give any of the kids respect?
Kirsty: Some yeah, who they liked. People who work at the subject, who was the brightest in the class, and like that.

Eva: And so what was different in the, in the higher groups?
Nahim: Teachers were quite serious, some teachers [I] used to have them for some lessons and they used to really care, but in the higher groups.
Eva: Right.
Nahim: They used to care a lot. They only liked people that would be clever. And people that don't know that much, they don't like 'em at all.

Nathan: She [Nathan's mother] didn't like none of them. The way they
           speak about the pupils. They put them all down. All of them.
           You got a few good ones, the ones that do well and they're all
           their chums.

In the last section we saw that the interviewees were sensitive to the
differences in teacher-student interactions generally. Here we see many
of them demonstrating an acute awareness of the differences in teacher
behaviour towards students of different status and also a sophisticated
understanding of the social system in place at school. Inter-relations in
the school are framed by a hierarchy of worth. The hierarchy, as understood by the interviewees, consists of teachers at the top, themselves at
the bottom, and 'more able' or 'better behaved' students in between. The
criteria for determining one's position in the hierarchy are entirely
school-defined. The recognised dimensions of importance are ability
and/or knowledge, and behaviour. Only a few of the interviewees
criticised the behaviour of students assumed to hold higher positions in
the hierarchy. As the above comments show, it is the differential treatment teachers demonstrate which attracts criticism.

The hierarchical relationship, at least that aspect which concerns
teachers and students on the lowest tier, is often compared to the parent-
child relationship. Comparing it to the private realm of home, the
behaviour of teachers is deemed inappropriate either because it assumes
the role reserved for parents or because it extends the boundaries of
appropriate treatment as established by families.

Yvonne: He got me that mad, I wanted to kill him. 'Cause I mean like,
           if I go home, no-one I know, none of my family, none of my
           friends, no-one I know shouts at me like that. It's only people
           who ever treat me like that, were a few teachers at that
           school. And nobody else did. I mean, even my own parents
           wouldn't shout at me like that. So no-one else has the right,
           that's the way I see it, no-one else has the right.

Tuscar: Yeah. It's like that, I don't think anyone should shout at
           anyone, like done wrong or not. ...
Eva: What would be a better way then?
Tuscar: I dunno, do what they wanted, but, start shouting at
           everybody and that. It's like, like if anyone should shout it's
           parents, so, that's what I think anyway.

Yaz: Because I just didn't like getting told what to do, I thought why should I get told what to do ... I used hate it when they [said], 'Do this, sit down and do this', I just used to hate it. 'Cause not even my mom spoke to me like that, and I thought, I ain't gonna let teachers speak to me like it.

Flattening the hierarchy and rejecting particular behaviours which reflect the power imbalance seemed of some significance to the young people and this was often expressed in terms of adult-child constructs. Finding themselves chronologically between the two, the interviewees aspire to the former and reject treatment deemed appropriate for the latter. This arose most often when they were comparing their previous school to their present Centre.

Yaz: ...I feel like an adult myself when I'm here, 'cause that's how the teachers teach you when you're here.
Eva: Right.
Yaz: They like, treat you like, you're one of them.
Eva: Oh yes.
Yaz: That's why I like it.
Eva: Really.
Yaz: You don't get treated like a little baby...

Gary: She was all right, I suppose. But she used to just get, she used to treat me like a child, and it used to get on my nerves.
Eva: Yeah, yeah. What sort of things would she do?
Gary: She just, like, explained things over and over again, and you already know what she's on about.

Nahim: ...the other school the teachers treat you like babies.
Eva: Yeah.
Nahim: This school they treat you, you like, not babies. They treat you like a normal person.
Eva: Right. Is that, is that important to you?
Nahim: Because they, you know, when you get in trouble they go, 'You're grown up, you're not supposed to be doing these things', and this and that. And then when you try and learn something they gonna call you babies or something like that, and say you act like kids...

The students' application of adult-child constructs further shapes our understanding of hierarchy as a framework. The young people view their treatment at the lowest tier of the hierarchy as suitable for children: autonomy, responsibility and, most importantly, respect are all lacking. Acquiring these qualities is associated with gaining adult status. In school, this status was reserved for teachers and possibly some students. Moving up the hierarchy to attain a more adult status seemed unachievable at school but many interviewees felt it was achievable in the Centres. It is not that the interviewees were better able to move themselves up a hierarchy but rather that the nature of the Centre social system was qualitatively different and the interviewees did not regard the Centres in terms of hierarchy. One of the effects of this is that a different set of teacher-student interactions emerged.

An ideal model of teacher-student relations

Students' relationships with teachers is a key feature of their experience of school and for many disaffected young people, these relationships are largely negative. It may be assumed from some of these accounts that interacting with these students may also be a negative experience for teachers.

The negative impact of poor or antagonistic relationships is likely to be felt well beyond specific interactions. For teachers, it undoubtedly contributes to overall levels of stress and potentially to burn-out. For young people it is linked to their self-perception and self-esteem. It is also linked to the likelihood that they will remain in school. O'Keefe and Stoll (1995) show that two-thirds of truants claim they truant because of lesson dissatisfaction. This dissatisfaction is derived from finding lessons boring or irrelevant, finding the work too difficult or the workload overwhelming, or *because they did not get on with the teacher* (p.13). Poor relationships with teachers may have a real and significant impact long after a young person's formal education is finished. Teachers are often the gatekeepers of the information, support and opportunities that help young people to make the transition from school to further study and/or the working world. Without this support the young people are likely to flounder (Stanton-Salazar, 1997).

How can relationships between teachers and students be improved? The accounts of the young people in this study provide some clear guidance on how to engage, rather than alienate, students. The interviewees' accounts of both mainstream and Centre experiences provide the basis for the construction of an ideal model of the teacher-student relationship. It is important to the interviewees that they feel cared for but they reject the *in loco parentis* model of care. These students, in their final years of schooling, do not express a wish for teachers to act as surrogate parents but seem rather to want a unique relationship in which their non-child status is recognised and responded to while, at the same time, their pastoral needs are met. The defining feature of the ideal teacher-student model, wherein teachers can communicate 'caring' without inadvertently 'parenting', is dialogue. Interviewees repeatedly mention certain teachers who *knew* them, who would *talk to* and *explain things* to them, and who would *listen*. The nature of the dialogue is such that the teachers' experience, knowledge and skills are shared and that the experience, knowledge and skills of young people are valued and contribute to the dialogue. This dialogue is essential in lessons as well as less formal situations.

There is one aspect of the young people's accounts, however, which contradicts their desire to interact according to this model. This is the matter of who takes responsibility for behaviour. The interviewees expressed a desire for teachers to speak to them 'proper' and 'kind', to treat them like adults and not children, and generally to recognise their ability to interact in a mature way. At the same time many of the comments imply that the young people feel that teachers should take the responsibility for the behaviour of them and their peers, evident in their call for the teachers to be stricter. Some young people want the teachers to be responsible for physically keeping other students away, whether particular individuals or the entire student body, by isolating the interviewee.

Dana: ...Could have just put me in a classroom on me own. I would have been happy.

Like most of the interviewees who experienced difficulty relating to peers, Dana felt the teachers could resolve her behaviour issues by preventing social interaction. Others wanted teachers to prevent them from misbehaving by offering diversionary activities such as using the computer or reading a book. The call for teachers to play a greater role in controlling student behaviour undermines the development of the ideal model of teacher-student relations discussed above. Rarely do the interviewees comment on the role of their behaviour in specific conflicts, or express a concern about the 'rightness' or 'wrongness' of their own actions. It is easy to see how this reluctance to assume responsibility for actions can lock students and teachers into interactions where the students are indeed treated like 'babies'. Can it be that the interviewees perceive the responsibility for their own behaviour to lie with teachers because the current system serves to infantilise young adults? The majority of the young people in this study consider themselves to be at the bottom of the school hierarchy. They have been identified as low-achieving, poorly behaved, or both, and have been offered little opportunity to share power and exercise control over their educational experience in a more adult-like manner. The default position for the interviewees to assume, then, is that of the child: dependent, powerless and not to be held responsible for their actions.

Rudduck *et al.* (1996) observe that '...the conditions of learning in the majority of secondary schools do not adequately take account of the maturity of young people, nor of the tensions and pressures that they experience...' (p.173). In advocating the model they do, the interviewees are demonstrating their capacity to interact on a more adult level. They recognise and value teachers' roles as educators and providers of pastoral care. In challenging the present model of teacher-student relationships, they are not calling for teachers to cease teaching or taking responsibility for discipline but are challenging the ways in which these responsibilities can be carried out. In this model, respect for individuals mediates teachers' actions in fulfilling their professional responsibilities. Teacher and student interact on an almost adult-to-adult level.

This 'ideal' model of teacher-student relations, based on the views of excluded students, is not an unrealistic goal. Already many of these students, who may be amongst those most disaffected from school, have experienced collaborative relations of power with teachers and valued these experiences. Particularly in the Centres, the interviewees report feeling respected as individuals and learners, cared for as young people, and valued. Relations of this type tend to have occurred too late in the interviewees' academic careers – after their permanent exclusion from mainstream school. The proposed model of teacher-student relations, based on the interviewees' accounts and views, can be read as an appeal for change. This appeal is driven by the often negative experiences of excluded students but is also informed by what these students consider to be teachers' 'good practice'.

5
Relationships with Peers in School

W hen young people speak of their experiences at school, a great deal of their dialogue revolves around their interactions with peers. In fact, 'peers' as a topic is second in salience only to interactions with teachers. This chapter is concerned with the interviewees' understanding of the peer world and their position within it. For the purposes of the present analysis, peers are considered to be any young people in the secondary school who are mentioned by the interviewees. Interactions with young people outside of school will be covered in the next chapter.

Two features of the interviewees' comments on peer interaction are striking. The first is the consistency in the young people's descriptions of the social atmosphere of school. They describe a peer world characterised by a sense of malice and ill-intention. Secondly, despite the consistency with which the interviewees describe the world of their peers, we see considerable difference in the way each of them managed peer relationships and, consequently, in their experience of their peers.

This chapter begins with the social atmosphere at school as described by the excluded students in this study and notes the predominance of fighting in the accounts, and the role conflict plays in determining social standing. Within this social environment we then examine the patterns of peer interaction experienced by young people – patterns that are distinctly different.

Social atmosphere

Phelan *et al.* (1994), in their study of a wide cross-section of young people in four US secondary schools, found that the students were mainly appreciative of their time spent with friends. They said that they could be themselves with friends and that friends provided a release from the pressures of school and family. In the UK, Cullingford and Morrison (1995) describe a very different peer environment among current young offenders. Peer relations for these young people were a source of strain and worry. In their paper on bullying in secondary school, Cullingford and Morrison comment that

> Rather than clear-cut cases of bullies, who can be isolated and dealt with, *there exists in schools an overall sense of gossip and malice.* (p.552) [*italics mine*]

The experience described by the young offenders in Cullingford and Morrison's study is akin to that described by the excluded students in this study. Although there was considerable difference in the way individual interviewees managed their relations with peers, the social atmosphere at school was consistently described as being rife with conflict. The descriptions of interactions in the classroom and, even more, outside lessons paint a picture of a volatile existence where emotional and psychological well-being is constantly under threat.

Social standing among the young people in this study was determined by an individual's ability to cause injury to another student, whether physical or, more commonly, emotional. Most frequently reported were intentionally hurtful exchanges of words and actions – commonly referred to as 'blazing'. Kirsty reveals how important these exchanges can be in determining an individual's social position relative to peers.

> Kirsty: It's like when you're outside with your mates, and all start like blazing each other, like saying things about each other, and like, one gets the better of you. You feel, it feels funny sort of. She's won ya; you're [a] looser and you're, like, you're dumb and everything.

The range of topics deemed suitable for 'blazing' is surprisingly broad. Often the comments focused on personal characteristics or aspects of private life over which the young person has no control.

> Sam: He said, 'At least my mom hasn't got fake valves.'
> Eva: Fake valves? what's that?
> Sam: You know the valves what are in your heart?
> Eva: Oh yeah.

Sam:	They bust, so they had to replace 'em.
Eva:	Ah, so they made fun of a condition that your mum has?
Sam:	So, I hit him, and done what I had to do.

Nathan: ...there was this one kid that always got beat up because he was really feminine and he was always with the girls. So he used to get beat up for being gay, but he wasn't gay. He was the one with all the girls.

Kirsty: What they wear, like got a hole in your jumper or something, or your trainers, 'What's the matter can't you afford a new jumper?' Like, you've got old shoes, you wear them like since like, in year eight, and you wore 'em since year eight till year nine, they go, 'You tramp, can't you afford new shoes?'

These comments touch on highly sensitive issues for the young people and are often very hurtful. At the same time, Kirsty's reference to winning and losing shows the importance of being able to operate in such antagonistic environments and being capable of generating retaliatory remarks. Failure to do so, at least in Kirsty's case, seems to diminish social standing and self-esteem.

Young people perpetuate the adversarial atmosphere in school in other ways too. Physical provocation, name-calling, stealing and staring or giving 'dirty looks' were common in the interviewees' accounts.

Charles: I called Tracy a Peck, and she'd cry.

Eva: What does a Peck mean?

Charles: It's just a small person. Cause she was a small person, we used to call her a Peck. And we used to call Louise a Beaver, cause she had big teeth. We used to call Sally Anne, Chip-Peeler, because of the way her teeth was. Used to call Sharon the Tramp. Honestly they used to start it because we'd walk past them or we'd be speaking in lesson and they'd say 'Shut up', and we'd say 'No', and they'd go 'Shut up, you tramp'....

Yaz: And I had my keys in my hands, and I was standing there waiting for my friends, swinging my keys, and um, there was one girl she walked out the toilets and she was staring at me. I thought just because it's my first day, I weren't just gonna let people take me for an idiot, stare at me and think that they're better than me. And she come out the toilets and I was standing there swinging my keys, and she stood in front of me, she went, she copied what I was doing...

Antony: And every morning ... I went in there, in the dinner room and didn't have any dinner, and he got away with my money...he was hitting me for no reason, punching me...

Other examples of antagonism of this kind were gendered and/or racialised.

Lorraine: It was, like sometimes like the boys would like touch me, or something, and I wouldn't like it.
Eva: Right.
Lorraine: So then I'd fight them, and then I'd get in trouble for that. Or sometimes the boys would get in trouble...

Tonya: Use to call you Black this and Black that, all that kinda stuff, and, you know. One of them called me Black this, Black that, I just kicked him from the top of the stairs, going down to the bottom.

As the quotes reveal, much antagonistic behaviour leads to physical fighting. Fighting is one of the most consistent school experiences across analysis categories. Thirty of the 33 young people interviewed reported physical fighting with peers. The term 'fighting' is used quite broadly: interviewees use it to describe intense verbal conflict with some intimidating physical behaviour (such as pushing), short-lived physical aggression and prolonged physical violence.

Both the frequency of fighting and its centrality to the interviewees' experience of school varied but most of them reported fighting to be relatively common and integral to their lives.

Sam: No, even if you get expelled, you don't stop fighting.

Tuscar: ... like what I got expelled for, that's a bit dummy. Like getting expelled for fighting and that ... everyone fights and that.

Given the universality of the experience of fighting, it is worth considering how fights take place and their social importance for the young people. There were two predominant types of provocation. By far the most commonly reported fighting appeared to erupt from immediate, antagonistic stimuli.

Eva: So, so at your school what kind of things would start a fight?

Carl: Um, I dunno, a few things, um like when we're playing football and ... like they score a goal and they say, 'Oh that wasn't a goal 'cause we weren't ready'. They just start fighting 'cause of that.

Yaz: 'Cause we was walking in the gates and um, she kept on treading on the back of my shoes.

Eva: Right.

Yaz: And I said um, 'Karen, move away from the back of my feet, stop trying to walk on me'. And she went, 'Shut up you div', and I just gone like that, behind me [thrown her pot noodle on Karen], and she slapped me ...

Other fights appeared to be more premeditated, as provocation occurred some time earlier. Long-standing antagonistic relations with one other student fall into this category. Conflict of this nature, where each episode of conflict builds on the previous one, was reported by six interviewees. Fights might be set off by immediate stimuli, but the root of the conflict has a longer history. In some cases it is the result of gossip.

Nathan: He said things about me to people and they happened to be my mates, so they told me. I had a fight on him.

Here the physical aggression is not an immediate response to perceived antagonistic stimulus. The eventual aggressor perceives the other party as wronging him or her, deems aggression to be an appropriate response, and a fight ensues when the opportunity presents itself or is created. A similar scenario occurs when fights are reportedly a method of planned intimidation, where the interviewee perceives him or herself as providing retribution to someone who has wronged a friend or family member.

Yaz:... this Asian [girl] used to always say to Jackie, my cousin, 'Ugh what do you wear short skirts for, what do you do this for, what do you do that for'. And it was up to her what she wanted to do. Jackie, cause she's not a girl to fight other girls or give ya mouth, she used to tell me, and I'd have a whack...

Richard: On the weekend, [he] smashed a glass. I was away. He smashed a glass, and [held it up to my girlfriend] and I can't

remember what he said to her. And he didn't realise that I
went to Somersville [school]. And when I seen him there I just
went mad – beat him up, and beat him up, and beat him up,
and I got suspended for two weeks.

The consequences for taking part in fights were mixed. On the one hand,
success in combat could result in increased social standing, as Joshua
reports.

Joshua: Like the kid that I had a fight on, he's supposed to like be one
of the hardest in the year you know them kind of things. One
of them kind of things. I used to beat him up so everyone must
have thought that I was quite hard. ... like the ones that hang
about with him, used to hang around with, used to speak to
me more. Tell me what they were doing, tell me to come out
tonight. They was interesting so I started to hang about with
them.

For Joshua, the ability to compete successfully in an aggressive environment earned him the right to enter into a particular social scene. This is
one of the perceived positive outcomes of fighting. There were also
negative outcomes. Certainly the inability to fight could lower social
status and evoke further antagonism.

Kirsty: Yeah, it's like, just say it's in our school, and like, I had a fight
on you..

Eva: Right.

Kirsty: In the next half hour, they might start calling me a pussy and
everything.

Eva: Oh really.

Kirsty: Things like that.

Eva: Wow, for losing a fight?

Kirsty: Yeah.

Jon: There's not a lot of choice, is there? Nothing you can do. It's
your environment around you as well, isn't it? It's like the area
you're in. I mean, you can't act like a, dunno, like a little wimpy
boy or something in a rough area, can you? 'Cause then
they're going to pick on you.

Eva: And what's bad about being picked on?

Jon: Well, it's horrible, I mean, you hear of kids hanging
theirselves, 'cause they're getting bullied in school, and that.
It's things like that, isn't it?

The social importance of fighting seems to outweigh the institutional risks involved in fighting in school. This remains the case even when the institutional consequences are significant. Twelve interviewees were permanently excluded for fighting and an additional three given fixed-term exclusions. Four fights caused the police to be involved. Three interviewees were charged in court with assault and one was given a police caution.

The unquestionable message arising from these accounts is that these young people perceive the social atmosphere at school to be adversarial and conflict-ridden. The accounts of physical fights might be inaccurate – for example, only three of the interviewees reported losing fights. This is statistically unlikely so one can assume a degree of bravado and consequent exaggeration in the accounts. Whether malicious and antagonistic interactions evolve into actual physical fights is less important than the interviewees' understanding of the social world in which they operate, which is that it is emotionally unsafe. Malice, conflict and antagonism are perceived to be the norm and all social actions, including the formation and maintenance of friendships, take place within this norm. Many of the young people operate from a defensive position and have to protect themselves from the potential distress and extreme discomfort caused by poor peer relations.

Yet within this near-universally described peer world, there is significant difference in individuals' described patterns of interactions with peers. Despite the consistency in the perception of a norm of malice which largely regulates the peer social world, there is great variation in the way in which the interviewees position themselves within it.

Peer relations

Some interviewees did seem to enjoy a fairly secure position in the secondary school within a relatively large and stable group of friends. Others described smaller friendship groups. Still others reported friendship groups characterised by internal friction. A significant minority of the sample reported extreme difficulty in their interactions with all or most of their peers.

Two dimensions of the young people's accounts reveal their relationship to the peer world. One is their perception of themselves as inside or outside the peer world. Those interviewees who perceive themselves to be 'insiders' speak of social events and activities as an integral part of their school experience. They use the term 'we' to describe actions and attitudes, reflecting their sense of a collective identity of which they are part. Young people who perceive themselves to be 'outsiders' are unable to cross, or are uninterested in crossing, the border into this world. They describe social interactions at school from the stand-point of an individual. The identity of self is distanced and separate from any group of peers. The degree to which interviewees perceive themselves to be inside the peer world varies, allowing the inside-outside dimension to be conceptualised as a continuum.

The other dimension which characterises the young people's patterns of interaction with peers is the level of comfort they experience in the peer world – a comfort-discomfort continuum. At one extreme are the young people who are highly orientated towards their peers and who perceive themselves to be integral to the social fabric of the school. At the other extreme are those who experience constant or near-constant conflict with their peers. At other points on the continuum are young people who experience internal conflict within established friendship groups or those who describe high levels of comfort with certain peers concurrently with equally high levels of discomfort with others.

By placing these two dimensions in relation to one another, the patterns of peer interaction can be characterised opposite.

A. Insider-Comfort. *Yvonne, Joshua, Carl, Michael, Danni, Neil, Manny, Shelly, Tariq, Wayne, Brendan, Craig, Tim, Damien.* A large number of interviewees described themselves as crossing the border into the world of peers with relative ease and success. Their friendship groups resided in school rather than in the neighbourhood, and their identities were intrinsically linked to these groups. Although almost all of them had experienced fights with other students, their descriptions of interactions with their friendship group generally conveyed a sense of comfort and belonging. The level of comfort experienced varied among the fourteen young people in this group. Two of them, Yvonne and Joshua, described themselves as immensely well-known and well-liked members of their peer group.

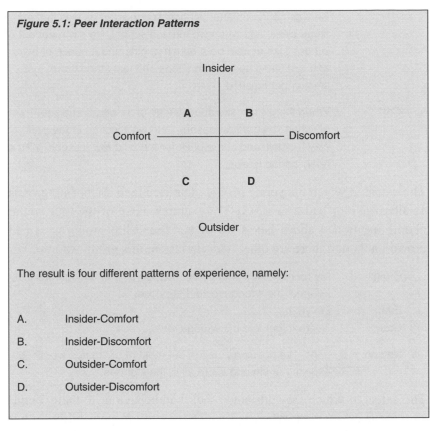

Figure 5.1: Peer Interaction Patterns

The result is four different patterns of experience, namely:

A.   Insider-Comfort

B.   Insider-Discomfort

C.   Outsider-Comfort

D.   Outsider-Discomfort

Yvonne: I had loads of friends, 'cause I was one of the popular bodies in my school. Everyone was my friend really.

Joshua: [explaining what he means by 'being safe' with the other students at school] Well, no-one trying to fight you or anything, or they wouldn't blaze ya or anything. And they'd say 'all right' to ya. And they'd say, 'Ya got any shirts, Josh?' or 'Ya got any shoes?' or sommat. Everyone would just come to you asking questions and you felt like 'Yeah, I'm the man', trying to show off.

Everyone in this group described social activities and events they enjoyed with their friends, recalling events in terms of 'we' and thus reflecting their sense of inclusion in the social scene.

Michael: But I wasn't bothered because all my friends were there, and we was still doing what we was doing, and talking about what we was gonna do after school. And most of us was in the same class, and when we meet in school, we still meet out of school. Like there'd be a bunch of girls and a bunch of boys, and just stand up, rob the shops and just stand there, just smoke, get mashed.

Carl: When there's um, like about fifteen of us will go and sneak out of school, wag a few lessons, and we'll just go in the park, play football, and come back for the next few lessons, if it's a really boring lesson.

The extent to which the young people identified their friendship groups as alternative or bad also varied. For example, none of the four young people mentioned above labels his or her friendship group as 'a bad crowd', although there are other interviewees in this group who do.

Craig: My mom knew it was gonna happen as well though. It's just, I dunno, the wrong crowd, I suppose.
Eva: Oh yeah.
Craig: Seem to get into the wrong crowd...

Nathan: ....no, like not being stupid, but most of my mates we all got expelled or left and we're all in the Centres.

The extent to which they attributed their bad behaviour to their friendship group also varied. Whereas Yvonne took full responsibility for her behaviour, referring to herself as 'the ring-leader', others said that their behaviour was heavily influenced by their peer group.

Michelle: Nah. We used to, like, say if it was in the lesson, we used to just sit there and then someone would, like, say something to us and then that's when, like, we'd start, like being bad and that.
Eva: Right. So when you would get in trouble, would it be when you were with your friends?
Michelle: Yeah.
Eva: Was it ever when you were just by yourself?
Michelle: Nah. When, uh, when I'm by myself, I realise then what I've done and that.

Manny: It would have been different Miss, if I just went to school Miss, depends who you're hanging around Miss that's the most important thing in school Miss. And like the right people Miss

	don't be excluded Miss for mixing with the wrong company Miss.
Eva:	Right.
Manny:	That's why you get excluded Miss.

The differences in the young people's perceptions of the influence of peers over their behaviour might signify differences in their levels of comfort. People who feel their behaviour is to some extent governed by peers may feel less comfortable and secure within the peer group than those who perceive themselves as in control of their behaviour. Two interviewees, Danni and Manny, reported a deterioration in their school friendships *after* their permanent exclusions. Danni talked about antagonistic relations with her former 'best friend' and Manny said that his school friends 'weren't bothered' about maintaining their friendships with him. This may indicate that these two individuals had more tenuous relationships and were less secure in their friendship groups than the other young people in this category. It can be said, then, that within the group whose crossing into the peer world is described as Insider-Comfort, there is some variation in the levels of security and comfort experienced.

B. Insider-Discomfort. *Lorraine, Kirsty, Leon, Nahim, Tuscar, Charles.* These young people also defined themselves largely in terms of their friendship group. They actively take part in social events and activities with a distinct group of friends and describe collective views and attitudes..

Nahim:	Used to do a lot of things that like, some grown up people only have fun, like that ... used to think of ourselves like um, grown up people that don't go school, don't go do exams or anything. Used to think like that.
Tuscar:	... like, we're all like the bottom group, and like, just, we'd all just have a laugh and that like...

Although they were a part of a social group of friends, the level of security they experienced in these relationships was very different to that of the interviewees mentioned thus far. Their friendships were characterised by discomfort and uncertainty. Their status in the group was uncertain and many of their described interactions with 'friends' were antagonistic.

Lorraine: It was like, it was like there was a group, and like, we'd all get together, sometimes they were talking to each other, and sometimes they weren't talking to each other. So I just always backed away from it, 'cause I didn't want to be in the centre. And then from then they thought, what's she going away for, and then they started on me. But I, but in a way I weren't really interested, but it really got to me.

Eva: How are they [your cousins] different from your other friends, your old friends?

Leon: They used to be in control. Like they said 'We'll do this, we'll do that,' you know. And like, my cousins discuss it before they go do it so it's like 'Let's do this' or 'nah, don't want to do this'.

Eva: And how is that different from your old friends?

Leon: They used to tell us. They used to go 'Go and do it'. They used to get me or someone else to get the blame and they just run off.

Kirsty: ...like when your friends make you dare, you've gotta do it, otherwise they call you like, chicken and nob and that kind of thing, and you get loads of hassle in school. You don't do something for them, [you get] clouted.

Eva: Oh, so what kind of hassle?

Kirsty: Start being bitchy with you, call you facey names and all that, I just call it them back. Just won't do what they tell me to do.

These young people operated with difficulty in the peer world. They showed a strong desire to be accepted and liked by their peers but their ability to interact successfully was limited causing them discomfort – often considerable – at school. Antagonistic relations can have strongly detrimental effects on the young person's educational experience.

Lorraine: ...all the trouble just got on me, and I weren't really interested in my work so much, because I was worried about 'Ah ... after next lesson it'll be break', and everything like that. Or I'd have to walk in the corridor and they'd say something to me.

Lorraine's tenuous position within her peer group was clearly a source of distress and interfered with her ability to engage in learning. The importance of belonging and the subsequent stress caused by conflict with friends is a defining quality of the interviewees in this group. It is this feature that distinguishes them most strongly from the next group.

C. Outsider-Comfort. *Jon, Perry, Gary, Yaz*. This group did not define themselves in terms of their peer groups at school. Interviews with them were characterised rather by descriptions of the self as completely independent of the school-peer context or even in contrast to peers. For example, Jon's involvement with a friendship group outside school was all-pervasive and he made little mention of peers at school. Perry, on the other hand, does describe many interactions with peers at school, but most are physical fights and he does not view himself as a member of a particular group but rather as an individual phenomenon.

Perry:	Um well, I went there like it was um, trouble there 'cause I went there with my reputation from junior school. Like I was getting into fights and everything, and um just fighting in general and beating people up, and like, it was like, and people looking at me when I was walking off, and whispering about me, 'Oh that's the kid who had that fight last week'. And at the time it was all right actually just walking around and every one knew ya. Yeah you know what I mean. Got a lot of respect now, you know what I mean.

Although Perry may perceive himself as having gained respect, he does not view himself as well-liked: 'I mean, most of the kids in my year hated me and I won't say otherwise'. Unlike the interviewees in the previous group, who would find this perception extremely distressful, Perry does not describe himself as feeling discomfort about the absence of positive peer relations. Yaz and Gary also view themselves as separate from their peers. Although they are able to establish friendships with some members of their peer group, they distance themselves from the main body of peers because they feel they are different from their peers because of their perceived greater maturity.

Gary:	They was all too immature, they didn't, they was all childish.
Eva:	Were they?
Gary:	Yeah.
Eva:	Right.
Gary:	And that used to get on my nerves as well.
Eva:	What kind of childish things did they do?
Gary:	Used to make stupid noises and like stupid things like that.
Yaz:	...the people in my year, there was nobody, there was just a couple of girls that I was going with, all the others there was

	just, they was too immature and they, I don't know what it was.
Eva:	Right.
Yaz:	But I used to hang around with boys because there was no girls who I could hang round with because they was divs really.
Eva:	Right.
Yaz:	Just too immature.
Eva:	Can you tell me more about what, what they did to be a div, or what a div is?
Yaz:	They just used to, they used to act like kids, act really young, like scream, and run up to boys, and say, 'Oh she fancies you'. You know the silly little ones.

This group differs from the other young people with Outsider experiences (Group D) in that one senses their lack of engagement in the peer group at school is a matter of choice. All describe comfortable relationships with peers outside school so it is not that they are incapable of successful interactions with peers but simply that they seem to elect not to engage in friendships with peers at school. Although both Yaz and Gary may feel annoyed by their peers, they seem secure and confident in their social standing in relation to them. Young people in the Outside-Comfort group do not describe the psychosocial discomfort associated over peer relations that is experienced by some of the other interviewees.

D. Outsider-Discomfort. *Antony, Dan, Dana, Richard, Sam, Sandra, Sarah, Tonya*. There was a significant minority of interviewees for whom interactions with peers were almost entirely antagonistic. These young people cited no particular friendship group to which they belonged. Although some described dyadic relationships with a romantic partner or a 'best friend', one sensed that they did not perceive themselves to be an accepted part of the overall social scene at school. The constant conflict they experienced with other students strongly shaped their life at school. They seemed to perceive themselves as incapable of harmonious interactions, describing themselves as 'easy to wind up'. They reported feeling 'picked on' and even 'tormented'.

Richard:	Yeah. Well it was like, everyone used to do it, but, everyone knew that I was the easiest to wind up, and used to go, 'oh if you wanna laugh, just go and have a go at Richard'. Used to come up, say something and have a fight, always.

Sandra: I don't know, 'cause people just pick on me for no reason. Like, you know, you pick on each other all the time, and I just start to fight then.

Sam: It was all right but, people just wanted to mess me around in there, so, to get me to fight and all that.

These young people find the border into the world of peers impenetrable, rendering them outsiders in the social life of the school. Further, they perceive the behaviour of peers towards them as strongly antagonistic and consequently experience great discomfort in their presence. Often this discomfort causes the young people to respond inappropriately to peer behaviour and this in turn reinforces their Outsider status.

Dana: Um, and this girl, she gave me a look and my first thought was, 'Go and pull her hair'.

Sarah: Yeah, other pupils, like, my friends like, but they knew that, if like I done something, if they said something to me, I'd start, and then like the teachers say something and they used to like me shouting at the teachers, so, they just used to enjoy it.

Eva: Right.

Sarah: So they used to wind me up.

Eva: And it was your friends who did that?

Sarah: Mm.

Eva: And what, did you think that it was okay for them to do that?

Sarah: No I didn't like it, 'cause like, I'd get into trouble, so. Wouldn't really quite like, it weren't, they weren't really friends, it was just like people who would speak to me in the classroom.

This aspect of the interviewees' personalities is reflective of the descriptions of 'rejected children' (Flavell et al.,1993; Price and Dodge, 1989) who display inadequate and biased processing of social cues (Price and Dodge, 1989, p.343). Whereas the previous group described seemed to express an element of choice in their Outsider status, these young people have not chosen to remain outside the peer social system at school but have instead been rejected by their peers, causing them great discomfort in the school environment

Transitions and trends in the interviewees' peer interaction patterns

The four patterns of peer interaction have been described as separate experiences but within the sample, there is evidence of some movement between pattern types. For example Yaz, who was placed in the Outsider-Comfort group as a result of her disdain for the student population in one school, described herself as getting on well with peers in another school. Lorraine experienced extremely distressing friction with a friendship group during her initial years at secondary school, which placed her in the Insider-Insecure category. At some point before her exclusion, these friends 'turned on' her and her subsequent sense of isolation was more like that of the Outsider-Discomfort group. Lorraine had a brief stint in a second school prior to her placement in the Centre, in which she described harmonious relations with her peers – another category. Another student, Jade, initially said that he 'got on with most of the kids in the class', but later in the interview said this:

Eva:	No, so did you know, um, were your friends, were they still in school?
Jade:	That's why I didn't really want to stay there, other people that was there , didn't really like them
Eva:	Right. And why weren't your friends in school?
Jade:	Got kicked out for fighting.

It seems that Jade was initially an Insider within a particular group of friends but that after these friends left school, he chose to stay outside the remaining peer group.

The most difficult transition would seem to be between Insider-Comfort and Outsider-Discomfort group. The former group is characterised by an orientation towards peers and a definition of self which is largely tied to a friendship group. Those in the latter group perceive themselves to be in a position of perpetual conflict with peers and most have a history of conflict that goes back to their primary school years.

Another difference between these two groups is their ethnic composition. Earlier it was noted that ethnic background cannot account for the differentiation in peer relations but that some trends do exist. Below is the interactional patterns matrix, overlaid with the names of the interviewees and their ethnic background and gender. Once the data is organised in this way, we see that certain ethnic- and gender-based patterns emerge.

The Insider-Discomfort and Outsider-Comfort groups are both fairly ethnically mixed. The other two groups, Insider-Comfort and Outsider-Discomfort, each include significant proportions of the sample and it is interesting to look at the ethnic composition of each. In the Outsider-Discomfort group, six of the eight interviewees are White-European, one is African-Caribbean, and one is of mixed parentage. This shows a disproportionate number of White-European students in this category – approximately 33% of all White-European students in the sample. In contrast, students from ethnic minority groups are under-represented in the Outsider-Discomfort group. For the purposes of this analysis, African-Caribbean, Asian and mixed parentage interviewees are grouped together as the ethnic minority sub-sample and only 13% are described as Outsider-Discomfort.

The Insider-Comfort group, in absolute terms, is evenly divided between White-European and ethnic minority interviewees (seven of each). Proportionately, this translates to almost 50% of the ethnic minority sub-sample, but only 38% of the White-European sub-sample. The experience of consistent, pervasive conflict with peers appears more likely to be an experience associated with White-European students. This suggests that the difficulties described by African-Caribbean, Asian and mixed parentage students are more likely to be related to features of the school experience other than constant antagonistic relationships with peers at school. These features include both relationships with teachers and factors outside of school that impinge on the school experience (discussed in the next chapter).

Another trend in the patterns of peer interactions can be found when the sample is analysed by gender. Of the twenty-three young men interviewed, fifteen (63%) described relatively comfortable relations with peers, and eight (29%) experienced discomfort. Only 40% (four of ten) of the young women interviewed described comfortable relationships, while the other 60% experienced discomfort. The female sub-sample is small, but this finding might indicate that excluded young women are slightly more likely to cite interactions with peers as a source of difficulty and distress in school, while young men are significantly less likely to report difficulty with peers as a primary source of distress.

Figure 5.2: Peer Interaction Patterns by Race and Gender

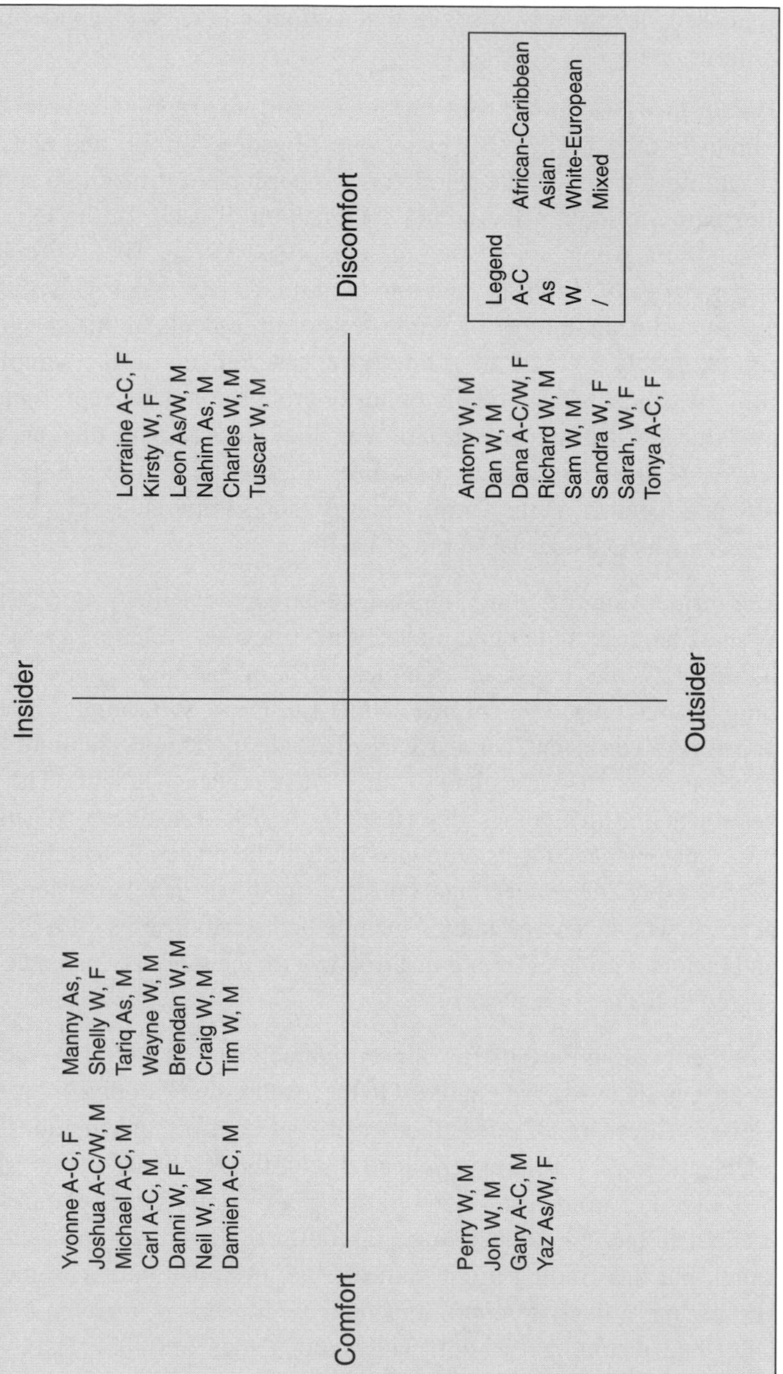

Insider

Discomfort

Lorraine A-C, F
Kirsty W, F
Leon As/W, M
Nahim As, M
Charles W, M
Tuscar W, M

Antony W, M
Dan W, M
Dana A-C/W, F
Richard W, M
Sam W, M
Sandra W, F
Sarah, W, F
Tonya A-C, F

Legend
A-C   African-Caribbean
As   Asian
W   White-European
/   Mixed

Outsider

Comfort

Yvonne A-C, F   Manny As, M
Joshua A-C/W, M   Shelly W, F
Michael A-C, M   Tariq As, M
Carl A-C, M   Wayne W, M
Danni W, F   Brendan W, M
Neil W, M   Craig W, M
Damien A-C, M   Tim W, M

Perry W, M
Jon W, M
Gary A-C, M
Yaz As/W, F

Conclusion

One of the most fascinating findings in the analysis of the young people's relationships with peers and peer groups is the distinct difference in the interviewees' patterns of interaction. For some young people friendship groups provide a sense of belonging and enjoyment, although there is notable variation in the extent to which this sense of belonging influences young people to engage in certain behaviours. For other interviewees 'friends' could be a source of friction and psychosocial stress, and for yet others, peers were a constant source of antagonism and could cause great discomfort.

There is a message here about individuality. It can not be assumed that all young people excluded from school find the same aspects of school to be difficult. Some of the young people found relations with peers extremely problematic. To have been effectively supported in school, their relationships with peers would have had to be addressed and measures taken to improve them. For other young people relations with peers were less problematic and support in school would probably have had to focus on other features of their school experience.

One aspect of the interviewees' accounts remained consistent throughout: the social world in which they interact with their peers is described as an aggressive, intimidating place. This is a particularly difficult problem to address, as it seems that much of the intimidating behaviour takes place when no school staff are present. Effective anti-bullying policies could do much to reduce the degree of malice felt by these students. More urgent than a focus on reducing individual antagonistic interactions, however, is a need to identify why such a social environment exists.

In the previous chapter we noted that the young people are acutely aware of the social hierarchy within the formal school culture and of their inferior position within it. Cullingford and Morrison (1997) note that when young people are rejected by the formal school system (i.e. the teachers), they may turn to friendship groups as a form of defence and a source of support outside the 'acceptable' peer culture (p.68-9). The authors comment on how the significance of these groupings can influence young people's behaviour, 'Recognising the importance of maintaining group solidarity, they may submit to pressure to conform to group norms and commit deviant acts...' (p.69). In the face of rejection from teachers and higher status peers, maintaining one's position in a friendship group would assume greater significance. Further, the group itself would be made up of peers whose self-confidence had suffered as a result of rejection, arguably resulting in a group of vulnerable young people. The result is a paradoxical situation in which the significance of the peer group in providing support is increased, while the individuals making up the group may be precisely those who are most vulnerable and least able to provide support.

This study shows that it is verbal and physical conflict that provide the interviewees with opportunities to exercise power and gain status within the peer world. Power must be exercised within the informal (peer) culture of school because there *is* no opportunity to do so within the formal (school) culture. To address the wide-scale bullying it is essential to look at ways in which more young people can be integrated into the formal school culture, not alienated from it. If young people feel valued and able to attain status and exercise some power within the formal school culture, they may not feel the need to exercise power in the peer world in the disturbing ways revealed in this chapter. The last chapter emphasised the importance of teacher-student dialogue, the key feature of which is valuing the experience, knowledge and skills of both teachers *and students*. The proposition here is that these dialogues taking place on a school-wide level would change the nature of the formal school culture by better integrating the qualities, skills and interests of all students. The outcome would be the reduction of the number of alienated young people and the amelioration of the conflict-ridden peer world associated with such alienation.

6

Factors Outside of School

Most of the conversation in the interviews revolved around events that took place in school and involved teachers and/or peers at school. Within these interviews however, a number of experiences outside of school were seen to impact on the school experience and this chapter focuses on these factors. The factors considered here are family, neighbourhood, involvement with the police and other compounding factors, such as drug and alcohol use and prolonged absence from school, focusing predominantly on the problematic aspects. Examination of difficulty and exclusion tends to highlight features of the excluded students' experience which were problematic rather than positive, particularly the influential factors outside of school. Outside influences were discussed in less detail than other aspects of their experience, such as relationships with teachers or relationships with student-peers. So if a young person raised a feature of their life outside school it was usually because it contributed in some way to their difficulty in school.

The significance of such factors to individuals' experiences varies greatly across interviewees. The home life of some young people or their involvement with neighbourhood peers or with drugs seriously impinged on their experience of school. For others, such factors played no significant role in their school life and did not feature in the interviews.

The nature of the data considered in this chapter differs from that of the previous two chapters. 'Relationships with teachers' and 'relationships with school peers' were the most prevalent topics in the interviews. All interviewees had something to say about these key features of the school experience and consequently a substantial proportion of the study is concerned with them and we can conclude that certain characteristics of school were experienced generally. Generalisations are made regarding the young people's views on the teacher-student relationship as well as on their accounts of the social atmosphere among the students in school. In this chapter, the experiences discussed are those of specific individuals in the sample. None of the factors outside of school mentioned are universally or near-universally experienced by the young people in the sample. The significance of this chapter is that it highlights the importance of the role that experiences outside of school *can* play in what happens in school.

Several of the young people reported some problematic aspect of their life outside of school, such as conflict with parents, violence in the neighbourhood and involvement with the police. Such aspects of their lives are among the many features that come together to shape the experience of school. In themselves, they neither cause nor are the result of problems in school, but factors such as family stress may contribute to the difficulty a young person experiences at school, just as conflict with peers or poor relationships with teachers can. There are a few interviewees for whom factors outside of school shape their school lives disproportionately, either during a particular episode in their school career or continuously. For example, a young person may become so involved with criminal activity, the police and the justice system that school life and formal education become comparatively insignificant. Each section in this chapter first considers how the relevant factor is reported to affect the young person's life generally and, second, discusses the specific cases of individuals who identify a given factor as having significantly affected their experience of school.

Family

In 1996, OFSTED undertook a study of 112 young people excluded from school. It included detailed information about the home and family circumstances of the young people. Among the problems experienced by the students in the sample were poverty, the need to look after sick or disabled parents, strained family relationships, absentee fathers, the involvement of older siblings in crime or drug abuse, physical or sexual abuse, and racism in the residential area, if not the school (p.10). Many of these themes were echoed among the young people in this study, although not all the interviewees opted to speak about their home life.

Those who did speak about their families and family relationships did so because these affected their time at school. Five young people spoke of the lack of contact with at least one of their parents, either because of the parent's work pressures or because the parent was absent.

> Anthony: ...my mom works hard and [is] always working. I don't blame her though, I'm not saying it is her that's doing it, not entirely, but like, my mom's working a lot.

> Lorraine: ...and my mom, like, 'cause she's not with my dad, and like um, I haven't seen my dad, and that was getting at me as well, 'cause everyone's, 'Oh I'm going to see my dad, and going to get some money'. I'm thinking, 'Oh, I can't do that, I wish I could do that'. And that was getting on my nerves as well.

Seven of the young people mentioned conflict with a parent. This conflict was usually described in one of two ways. There were episodes of conflict – 'bad patches' – or there were antagonistic relations between parent and child which were described as chronic and continuous.

> Sarah: ...I can't control my temper and that. I've run away from home a few times as well. Because I've, I dunno, I just don't like being, like, locked up in the house, and if I do something, my mom will say 'You've got to stay in today', and I don't like it, that's why I run away from home. She used to keep me in, and that. Um, [once] I ran away from home and she grounded me for a month. And after a week, I just got so wound up that I had to go again, I went again. And then when I come back she was all right, she said ... 'I'll let you go out,' she said, 'but, you, you've gotta come in earlier'. So I had to go in a bit early, but it was better than being stuck in the house.

> Eva: How, how important is ... what your mom thinks to what you do?
> Craig: It is important ... I don't get on with me dad very well, so like, I always depend on my mom.

Other difficulties at home affect some of the young people's lives. Two of the interviewees, Nahim and Sam, mentioned the poor health of their mothers. Related to this, particularly in the case of Nahim, was poverty. He spoke of poverty-related issues which shaped his life.

Nahim: ... like if you had a good job and everything we'd be living, you know we have a normal life. But we have to, like, go out of the way to get, to get the food for the house and everything.

Five young people spoke of the fact that either they or a sibling had spent some time living away from their parents' home(s). Although none explicitly mentioned family difficulty, the separation from parents may have been indicative of strain in the family at that time.

Importantly, difficulties at home cannot be held completely responsible for disruptive behaviour at, and exclusion from, school. Phelan *et al.* (1994) found that 26 of the 55 mixed-ability students they interviewed in the US described family stress. Nineteen of the twenty-six maintained passing grades at school (p.436) so although issues such as poverty, poor parental health and absent parents are likely to make life difficult for a young person, these disadvantages cannot be held solely accountable for poor behaviour in school. Although several of the young people describe disadvantageous home circumstances, it is not suggested that these are the causes of disruptive behaviour in school.

In fact many of the young people explicitly highlighted the support they received from their parents, both specific help and encouragement to achieve academically, and general emotional and moral support.

Carl: Like I'm getting better grades here, and when she [mother] went to town yesterday she bought a sweater for doing quite good here as well.

Lorraine: Yeah, I did have a lot of support from her.

Eva: Is that important to you?

Lorraine: Yeah it is, because some people don't have it. Some people don't have it, some people are unlucky. I mean, the thing with my mom, she don't compare to others. And she don't compare herself to now-a-days like ...'When I was younger, I couldn't do this and I couldn't do that'. Or, 'Look at that girl, look how well behaved she is and look at you'. She doesn't do stuff like that.

Michael: What dad's trying to do for me is make everybody know that I'm not a bad person. Really I'm a good person and I can do well. So when I'm up here and I'm getting a good grade, he's feeling happy, telling people [in their home town] that, 'He's not as bad as you think'.

The majority of the young people interviewed apparently felt that their parents cared for them and wanted them to do well. Many stated that they continue to attend the Centres and try to achieve because it is important to their parents. Several said that they stopped taking part in or avoided criminal activity because of the distress their involvement had caused or would cause their parents.

Two facets of 'family background' can impinge on difficulties at school – a disadvantaged socio-economic background and the impact of family crisis and/or vulnerability. It is nonetheless difficult, and arguably futile, to try to determine a causal relationship between family background and difficulty in school. Indeed, Galloway (1985) found that although free school meals (as an indicator of family socio-economic background) correlated strongly to persistent absences, it did not correlate significantly to exclusion from school (p.51). Rather than hypothesise about the relationship between the disadvantage that some of the young people describe and their difficulties in school, it is more enlightening to examine the accounts of certain young people who speak explicitly about the interaction between their family and school lives.

Three interviewees in this study perceived family crisis to be the cause of a disruptive incident at school. Gary, who was excluded on a fixed-term exclusion from primary school, told me:

Gary:	...the worst one I hit a teacher. That was in junior school, and I regretted that.
Eva:	Yeah.
Gary:	So they let me back in. They thought it was a one-off.
Eva:	Right, what happened in that case?
Gary:	... Nothing, just told me to come back in the school and just, like, calm down a bit. It's because my mom and dad split up that's what made me do it, and I blew up.

Kirsty attributes her 'playing up' largely to the separation of her parents, while Lorraine cites the death of her grandmother as the catalyst for conflict at school.

Lorraine:	...my grandma died the day before, just a day before.
Eva:	Right.
Lorraine:	And um, I didn't have to go to school, but I didn't want to miss out, 'cause I mean, everyone's gotta go but, it was like, I

couldn't [miss]. And then I went to school, and they was just like saying things and like it was really getting on my nerves, and saying, 'Oh, she's getting cheeky now, she's getting cheeky'. And then the fight just happened...

Kirsty:	... Part of the reason why I messed up in school, it's like mom and dad got divorced.
Eva:	Oh.
Kirsty:	So like, it really upset me, and this...
Eva:	Yeah.
Kirsty:	Missed school a lot, and all this about me mom, used to go out drinking and everything, coming in late.
Eva:	Right.
Kirsty:	Didn't care about school...

Two other interviewees commented on the relationship between their family life and school in another way, describing conflict at school not as a result of a crisis in the family but rather as connected to the static, long-term vulnerability in their home lives. In the last chapter, Sam spoke about the conflict evoked by a peer who teased him about his mother's medical condition. For Richard, it was the absence of his father that triggered his sensitivity and caused conflict and fighting at school.

Richard:	...most of the things in the junior school what started me off was, people mentioning things about my dad ... Start fighting 'cause of what they said. I didn't even know why I done it 'cause ... my dad left me, he didn't die or anything, he left me. He left my mom before I was even born. Just selfish and horrible, and I don't know why I stuck up for him ... Everybody else just tended to get on with it like, and that, but me with a chip on me shoulder, to protect someone.

In the case of both Richard and Sam, the vulnerability they felt in their family lives made them particularly sensitive to the taunts of their peers. The ensuing conflict between themselves and peers caused teachers to intervene and led to disciplinary measures against them.

All the difficulties young people and their families face, ranging from socio-economic factors such as poverty, to family crises such as death or divorce, affect their lives. These are factors which contribute to their overall experience of school. In many cases we are left to assume a relationship between family life and school life – that it is difficult to believe that poverty, illness, and conflict at home would not affect young people, even if they do not identify a relationship between such factors and experiences of school. In other cases the links are more explicit. Phelan *et al.* (1994), write: '...nearly 50% of the students reported that family conflicts impinge negatively on their psychological well-being, interfering, more or less frequently, with their ability to concentrate in school' (p.435). This finding certainly reflects the experience of the five interviewees whose accounts make clear to us how home life intersects with school life and can cause difficulties in school.

The neighbourhood

The influence of the neighbourhood is not a wholly separate issue. Experiences in the neighbourhood might include involvement in crime (discussed later), interaction with peers not from the school (and usually older), or racism. The experiences cited here have been noted and grouped together as 'neighbourhood' because they are significant features of the interviewees' experience which take place neither in the school nor in the home and, for the most part, involve some interactions with individuals living in the same area.

Several of the interviewees described themselves as coming from 'rough areas', or from neighbourhoods where there are many school-age young people not attending school.

Eva:	Mmm. Do you have any friends that have been expelled?
Tim:	From my school?
Eva:	Any school.
Tim:	I think most people around my area where I live...
Eva:	Mmm.
Tim:	Most of the kids my age like they don't go to school – it's not worth it or they've been expelled. They either here or are at [another Centre].

Tim's comment, like those of several others, does not make explicit a relationship between neighbours and his difficulties in school but it does suggest the culture of the neighbourhood may not be congruent with the culture required for success in school.

The way in which neighbourhood variables affect an individual's school life varies. For Nathan, conflict with neighbours resulted in conflict at school.

> Nathan: Yeah...and because I know the dinner ladies as well live by me. And because no-one in my area likes me either they didn't so in the school, they carried it on in school.
>
> Eva: Oh right.
>
> Nathan: So that then the teachers started 'cause I was being all assy to the dinner ladies and the teachers had to get involved and take sides with the dinner ladies.

The conflict Nathan experienced with the dinner ladies was one of many he experienced at school. Although not the central feature of his educational experience, it was significant enough for him to consider that moving from the area was a positive change, as he later told me.

> Nathan: I don't like the [new] area, but I like some of the people in it
>
> Eva: Who are the people that you like?
>
> Nathan: The neighbours and that.
>
> Eva: Oh yeah.
>
> Nathan: They're old, all of them – I think we're the only kids there – but they're all nice.
>
> Eva: That's good. So it's better than the dinner ladies.
>
> Nathan: Mmm.

Nathan's relationships with neighbours affected his experience at school both directly and indirectly: directly when specific conflicts were brought from the neighbourhood into the school and indirectly by influencing his general sense of comfort in school. He discussed the move in the context of the various factors which contributed to his success at the Centre at the time of interview. The move to a new, more amiable neighbourhood was noted as one of several influencing factors.

The majority of the interviewees who mentioned their neighbourhoods referred predominantly to their neighbourhood peers. Sandra describes her on-going difficulties with some of her neighbourhood peers as well as her response to their antagonistic behaviour.

> Sandra: There's a gang after me still, in my area, yeah. You know gangs on the street or anything.
>
> Eva: Yeah.

Sandra:	Start bullying me, like, and that sort of thing. But, I just walk off, or try and avoid 'em.
Eva:	Yeah. Who are they, the gangs?
Sandra:	I don't know who exactly who they are. Some of 'em, are from [former school], like you know, and start messing around, and fight. You know the sort of things. And they've got in a gang, and start bullying me now. They know my name and everything.
Eva:	Right.
Sandra:	Every time I see 'em, I just like, try and walk across the road, or something. So they won't see me.

Although Sandra does not attribute her difficulties in school specifically to her neighbourhood peers, bullying is a central theme of her experience and takes place at school and in neighbourhood life. She cites her problems with peers as the predominant factor in her difficulty at school.

The image of youth in economically disadvantaged areas suggests gangs in the streets bullying others (as described by Sandra), or criminal activity. For several young people there existed an opportunity and/or pressure to take part in 'street' activities such as crime or violence. Some young people, however, actively resist involvement, as the following interviewees describe:

Eva:	Yeah, and did some of the kids that you hung out with did they get into trouble outside school?
Joshua:	No, because I didn't used to go outside. We used to go round to my friend's house and there be about eight of us in his house and we used to just stop in his house, watch telly. None of us touched drugs because, like, we all wanted to play football.
Craig:	It's just all my friends, they're all interested in cars. And, I dunno, I dunno, 'cause I wanted a car, as soon as I could, because, um, there's a lot of joy riders round by us, and you see cars going around all the time.
Eva:	Yeah.
Craig:	... so I stayed away from it, but, like, I dunno. I think it's only a matter of time before I just, you know what I mean, start doing, start doing that. Because, if I got a car of my own, and got something to work on, or something like that, know

	what I mean. Nothing, I mean I'm not gonna be bothered with any other cars, am I? But, I mean my brother got caught up in that joy riding.
Eva:	Yeah.
Craig:	And like, he, he nearly went down and that. So um, so I sort of... Mom's always been against it, so I didn't want to put her through what she went through with my brother.

These interviewees consciously resist the opportunities presented to them to take part in illegal activity but there are others who are swept into street activity. Several report taking part in some sort of criminal activity or street fighting, in some cases entirely outside the school. Others consider their involvement in street activity to be one of the many factors contributing to their difficulty in school. Two interviewees, Jon and Perry, describe themselves as highly involved in 'street' life, which means much more to them than anything else in their lives, including school. Other life factors such as teachers, school peers, and family seem to pale in significance compared to their lives with neighbourhood peers.

Through his neighbourhood peers, Jon became involved in car crime.

Jon:	You just hang around the street and, I don't know, you feel kind of forced to do things, like steal a car, or something. And you just go along with them and you steal a car and have fun and all that. And you do the things they do, then you're alright with them. But now, like, I've stopped. And now that I've stopped, they're alright still, but they're a little bit funny like, 'Jon, you want to come get a car?' 'I don't do it no more'. 'Oh right then, see you later', and off they go somewhere else, or something.
Eva:	So you felt forced?
Jon:	Mmm. Well not forced, no, 'cause I've got a mind of my own, but you want to do it, just to be in the gang, like, you know, be one of them or something.

Jon seemed to see his identity as intrinsically linked to his involvement in street activity. It separated him from other young people his age and made him feel unique.

Jon:	...But I still hang around, like around the streets and all that with them [old friends].

Eva:	Right. Do you think they'd be OK with you, if you hadn't originally gone with them?
Jon:	No, because then I would sort have been, a normal boy, wouldn't I? Stuck in the house or something, or go out with your mum and dad. Not very fun is it?
Eva:	So, is that what a normal boy is like?
Jon:	Yeah, you just go out, and visit your aunt or something, don't you? It's boring. If you're out on the street, you've got things to do.
Eva:	Right. So, so it almost sounds like for you, going out, and getting in with that crowd, and sort of nicking cars and stuff, that's fun?
Jon:	It's fun, yeah. It was fun, I mean driving cars and all that on the road, and getting in police chases and that. It was fun, but it was scary as well...

Jon reports that the consequences for this type of activity became very serious for him when he was arrested on several charges.

Jon:	Well, I've been in cells before like, but, then, for like, such a serious crime, 'cause we'd like smashed into police cars, to get them out of the way, and caused injury to police officers, and all that, like putting other people's lives at risk. And I knew it was serious then. So, that's when I thought I was going to go away.

By then Jon was already permanently excluded from school and attending a BSS Centre. The Centre intervened by providing Jon with a placement assisting a police officer who was working with the Centre as part of a community project, providing outdoor activities to young people. At the time of the interview, Jon reported that he was no longer involved in car theft.

Perry was also highly involved in street life. For him, life revolved around violence, and the fights that determined the hierarchy among young male peers.

Perry:	Well, you go out into the street, right, you pick your biggest geezer on the street and you think, 'Oh this is gonna be the hardest one for me to beat'. Go and pick a fight with him, everyone's watching ya, 'Oh you know that big geezer, that big geezer there, he's hard to move, that little kid is there'. So

> the little kid ends up beating him, putting him in on his bum like. And everyone's like that, 'Oh that little kid's a fighter, look at the size of him' and all this, so um, ya know like that. And then once you're like that, 'Oh he's a good fighter he is, ya don't mess with him ... he's coming over to talk to ya'. When they've got respect for ya, you, you walk through a crowd of people and all that, none of 'em say nothing to ya. Just walk straight through like that. 'Alright, alright, alright'. Know what I mean?

Like Jon, Perry's identity is strongly tied to his participation in street activity. At the time of the interview Perry, age 14, was still deeply into this lifestyle.

> Perry: I went to a night club last night, it was exactly the same as school man, all moody crews up in the corners and everything. You know what I'm saying? See what's happened with these people nowadays, they think they're big men at the age of fourteen, fifteen and sixteen, they're going on like they're gangsters at twenty one, twenty two, twenty three, you know what I'm saying...

Perry's experience was compounded by a number of factors including stress in his home life, involvement in crime, and substantial use of drugs. Of all these factors, male violence was by far the most salient theme in his account of his school and life experience. Accounts of fights dominated his description of life both inside and outside school. Violence dominated both these worlds and little distinction was made between the two.

Another type of street conflict affected one sub-group of the sample. Three of the four Asian young men (including one of mixed parentage) described inter-Asian conflict as shaping their lives inside and outside school. The dynamics of these conflicts were complex, as the accounts of these three students reveal. Several of the interviewees mentioned the division between those of Pakistani and Bengali origin. Nahim, of Pakistani origin, describes his surprise at the helpful intervention of an Indian peer during a fight and then goes on to describe the racial divisions which shape his world.

Eva:	Right, and one Indian boy did? And he pushed him [the aggressor] out of the way?
Nahim:	It's unusual for those two together. I don't like it like that, but like Muslims stick with Muslims and black people stick with black people..
Eva:	Oh. Is he a Muslim? This boy [you were fighting with], was he...?
Nahim:	But not Muslim, Pakistani.
Eva:	Ah.....and Bengalis?
Nahim:	Yeah, Pakistanis and Bengalis. They're two different kinds.
Eva:	Countries, yeah.
Nahim:	Two different countries and two different kinds of people.

Manny, also of Pakistani origin, describes an incident precipitated by Pakistani-Bengali conflict.

Manny:	Then the next day there were more of them, Miss. It was dinner time, Miss, and I went to the shop, Miss. The shop was full of Bengalis, Miss, and I got my head kicked in, Miss, good and proper, Miss.
Eva:	Right, did you know these boys from school?
Manny:	No Miss, only some of them come to school, Miss. Just some of them don't go to school, Miss. They haven't got anything better to do.

These students speak of intra-Asian conflict but this is not to say that this was the only form of racism affecting the young people in the sample. Indeed some White-European interviewees expressed racist views, African-Caribbean interviewees described experiences of racism and Asian interviewees described inter-racial incidents. Intra-Asian conflict is highlighted here because these young men mentioned it repeatedly in their discourse and it appeared to be a highly significant aspect of their lives.

For Manny, Leon and Nahim racial conflict and violence appear to be the backdrop against which they conduct their daily lives. They can be described as having been relatively engaged in school life, showing some concern about their academic progress, and they talk of a social network of friends within the school. Although Leon said he had been involved in gangs and Nahim relates his part in a series of illegal activities, they also appear to think of themselves as students in school, an experience which has engaged them to a certain degree. In comparison, the street activity of Jon and Perry is their life. During each interview – the focus of which was school and exclusion – the dominant feature of these young men's experiences during their years at school was their involvement in crime and fighting, respectively. They can be described as socially disengaged from school and they scarcely mentioned schoolwork or academic concerns or aspirations. School seemed incidental to their primary concern with street life. Unsurprisingly, these two made far fewer comments about teachers and school peers than other interviewees did, since school generally seemed to be unimportant to them.

Crime

Twenty-one of the interviewees reported some involvement with the police during their educational career. Unlike Jon, for whom car theft was a way of life, most of them spoke about specific and often isolated incidents, which ranged from being stopped on the street for behaving suspiciously or fighting, to arrest, court cases and criminal charges. One young woman explicitly said that she had received a caution and another was on a supervision order at the time of the interview.

Interestingly, the proportion of crime-related activity that intersected with school life was relatively small. Three young people reported that they had been caught selling drugs in school, leading to permanent exclusion for two of them. Two young people reported police charges for trespassing/suspicion of trespassing on school grounds after school hours. As a result of the damage done in one case, one of them was excluded. Two young men reported stealing school property and one of them was permanently excluded for doing so. Finally, one young man was excluded for possession of an illegal weapon. In most of these cases, and in some cases of fighting, the school responded by bringing in the police. Unlike the pervasive involvement in criminal activity described by Jon, the incidents described by the interviewees seem to be manifestations of other significant problems in their lives.

Nahim's involvement in theft seemed directly related to the poverty in which he lived:

Nahim:	When I never used to have any money I used to get bored, 'cause you had to like steal something to get some money, innit.
Eva:	Mm.
Nahim:	Or we used to steal a car tape or something like that.
Eva:	Right.
Nahim:	Used to steal money out of a car, but we never used to go joy riding.

Leon's possession of illegal weapons is due to involvement in street gangs in his area.

| Leon: | It was mostly firearms and, like, they got caught with weapons sometimes and I took the blame for that once or twice. |

Leon's situation was similar to Richard's and Kirsty's – who were excluded for selling drugs – and Wayne's – who was excluded for trespassing and damaging property – in that these activities all took place in the company, and arguably under the influence of, older friends. All four of these young people were permanently excluded from school for their actions, showing clearly how friendships with older peers outside of school affect school experiences. Although not all four attribute their behaviour to the influence of these peers, the friendships do seem to influence the young people's actions and, when the actions take place at school, their educational experience.

Two of the interviewees related their involvement with the police and court system directly to their difficulties at school. Gary describes a lengthy court procedure which weighed heavily on his mind. He was being charged for causing injury to another young man during a fight.

Gary:	... Well yeah because at that time when I got expelled I had a court case on my back, and that was doing my head in.
Eva:	Right.
Gary:	I don't think if that was there, like court, nothing would have happened.
Eva:	Right, so how did that affect you in school?
Gary:	'Cause I had to go to the court and like the police were stressing me and that, and like all that sort of stuff.
Eva:	Right, and you...
Gary:	And the kid's parents like, phoning my house up saying, I ain't, we're gonna get sent down and all this rubbish.

Eva: Really.

Gary: Yeah, it was doing my head in.

Gary's involvement with the court system was compounded by antagonistic behaviour from another family in the neighbourhood and the resulting 'stress' influenced his schooling. Lorraine's interaction with the police because of her involvement with a street robbery was one of many factors in her life which contributed to her reaching crisis point at school.

> Lorraine: Mm that's it, and I have to keep on going to court for that as well. And that was, my mom was going down as well because – she didn't feel ashamed of me – it's like, um, because she was like grieving over my grandma as well. I got in trouble with the police as well, and like, my little brother he was getting in trouble as well. All of us just getting in trouble. And like, my mom's a single parent, as well.

Just as a strained family life can cause stress for a young person, so can involvement with the police. Practically and emotionally, legal procedures can consume much time and thought. It is easy to see how these procedures might cause a great deal of stress which can, in turn, precipitate additional conflict in school. In an earlier section we saw how the difficulties Lorraine experienced in her private life were cited as a catalyst for the fight at school that led to her exclusion.

Compounding factors

In some cases, a number of factors combine causing extreme difficulty, as Gary recounted. Two compounding factors considered next are drug and alcohol use and prolonged absence from school.

Several of the interviewees mentioned using alcohol or drugs at some time, mostly with peers and outside school hours. Three interviewees reported that using drugs and/or alcohol interfered directly with their school life. Kirsty's account earlier described how when her parents were getting divorced, she was going out drinking in the evenings and consequently could not get up for school in the morning. Nahim reports having regularly used cannabis and alcohol during school hours, as well as experimenting with heroin. He describes a period when he was drinking on a regular basis during school time.

Nahim:	And then afterwards we start wagging it. There was this one um, like um, off-license. You know what off-licenses are?
Eva:	Yeah, yeah.
Nahim:	We used to go there and the guy used to go out with me, and we used to buy beer and everything, and Bacardi and that.
Eva:	Right.
Nahim:	And he goes to me, he goes, I know a place where you can get free bottles, so we're wasting money here. So, you know everyone used to go up there we used to go to the brewery and we used to nick bottles from the back.
Eva:	Right, so how often would you drink in a week?
Nahim:	Every day.
Eva:	Really?
Nahim:	For about four months we used to drink every day.

Perry describes using amphetamines at school from a very young age.

Perry:	I used to be quite messed up on um, some mad drugs at that time as well. Used to go into school tripping and shit like that, man. And used to do loads of like whizz before I went into school.
Eva:	Oh right.
Perry:	I used to take loads of whizz before going to school and smoked some draw. Took whizz all the way through my year seven exams.
Eva:	Did you?
Perry:	Yeah, and I was only eleven, you know what I mean?

Nahim's heavy use of alcohol ceased when his mother discovered it. Perry did not comment on his use of drugs at the time the interview was held, but did say it became worse after his exclusion. Both Nahim and Perry live lives compounded by difficulties such as poverty, racism, the criminal activity of older male relations in Nahim's case, and street violence and the departure of Perry's father to live elsewhere. Substance use and abuse seems to be one of many features of these young men's lives which contributed to difficulty in school.

Extended absences from mainstream school were also cited as influencing school experience. All the interviewees described a time lapse between their permanent exclusion and placement in the Centre and several described prolonged absences from school at an earlier stage. There were a variety of reasons: Richard reports being permanently excluded in Year Seven and later re-instated. Because the appeal process took some time he was absent from school for a long time.

> Richard: I've missed about a year of school. But more than that including wagging it as well.

Richard highlights another reason for missing school: truanting. Several interviewees reported truanting over long periods.

> Kirsty: ... 'cause I used to spend a lot of time away from school ... I didn't want to go, 'cause I hated it.

> Joshua: ... that's what I usually do, just go round to someone's house and have a laugh. But it weren't funny because I weren't going to school, I was wagging school ... it's just, I didn't want to go to school because I felt that the teachers were getting at me.

For some young people, truanting became a way of life. Joshua describes truanting for two months before his mother found out and he began attending more regularly. There were other reasons for prolonged absences from school that were beyond the control of the individual. Yvonne was absent from school on account of her poor health and Leon was abroad during the first months of secondary school.

> Yvonne: And like in second year, 'cause I missed out a lot of school, 'cause I was in hospital, like end of the first year, second year...

> Leon: ...I never started the school from the beginning. I went abroad, you see, to Pakistan for a year.
> Eva: Oh yeah.
> Leon: And I came back and I was half way between first year when I started.

None of these absences are cited as the cause of difficulty in school, but they are probably disruptive and make it more difficult to achieve academically. Absence also limits the opportunity to develop and foster positive, supportive relationships in school with both teachers and peers which, as we have seen, are of paramount importance to young people.

Conclusion

OFSTED (1996) studied the cases of 112 students who had been excluded from school, 42 of them permanently. Among the difficulties faced by this group, OFSTED listed the following: poor acquisition of key skills, particularly literacy, limited aspirations and opportunities, poverty, family stress, poor relationships with peers, parents and teachers, and pressure from other students to behave in a manner likely to result in conflict with authority (p.10). All these factors are evident in the study sample. They are bound to affect the young people's sense of self and, consequently, their school experience. Masud Hoghughi, writing for the *Times Educational Supplement* (12.2.99), comments on the roughly 15% of students who come from families 'beset by poor health; unemployment; distress caused by poverty; poor relationships; predatory neighbours and weak community ties', and the subsequent poor mental health of the parents in these families (p.15). He observes that,

> Such families are unable to provide 'good enough parenting'. Their children do not receive adequate physical, emotional and social nurture or protection from harm. They are brought up without sensitive, internally-controlled behavioural standard, and so they acquire little idea of their own potential and how to fulfil it. These families do not have the motivation, resources or opportunities to help their children benefit from schooling. (*TES*, 12.2.1999, p.15)

Clearly, family circumstance impacts strongly on the young person's experience of school and, where disadvantage is endemic, seriously limits opportunities for engagement and success in school.

However, the temptation to suggest that the socio-economic and family background factors of the young people in this study cause their difficulty in school will be resisted for two reasons. For one thing, there is ample evidence that school factors have a strong influence over student behaviour, regardless of the socio-economic catchment area (OFSTED, 1996; Reynolds, 1976; Galloway, 1985; McLean, 1987). Although poverty and ill-health doubtless hinder parents' ability to promote their children's well-being, this research suggests that young people's socio-economic background cannot be held totally accountable for the difficulties they experience in school. Moreover, some of the interviewees did not report difficulties outside school. Neither family stress nor involvement with the police nor drug use were universal amongst the sample.

Instead of trying to determine the extent to which factors outside of school affect behaviour in school, it is far more useful to look at how these factors can influence the young people's lives at school. The interviewees' accounts provide specific examples of ways in which various life factors and events intersect their experience of school and cause difficulty. By examining these accounts, we gain insight into the dynamic interplay between various factors in the lives of the young people.

Gary, Kirsty and Lorraine illustrate how family crisis can cause emotional stress that results in conflict with teachers and school peers. Sam and Richard show how sensitivity about their vulnerable home situations contributed to conflict with peers. Other young people talk about how their involvement with the police could distract them from school life. Jon and Perry provide cases where the school experience can become completely overshadowed by and subordinated to experiences outside the school. Several of the interviewees described multiple difficulties outside school. Nahim experienced poverty, family stress, racism, drug abuse and involvement in criminal activity. Perry spoke predominantly of his involvement in street violence, but also about drug abuse, criminal activity, and the absence of his father. A number of factors contributed to Lorraine's crisis, including the death of her grandmother and participation in a street robbery that consequently involved the police. The lives of some young people seem manic, either episodically or permanently, with so many sources of stress needing to be managed at any given time. It is easy to see how such a situation could negatively affect a young person's experience of school.

The life factors covered in this chapter intersect the experience of school in a number of ways, and can be the very cause of exclusion, as in the case of drug dealing or possessing an illegal weapon. For others, situations outside the school create stress which is brought into the school and this stress can contribute to young people behaving confrontationally with teachers and peers. How much outside pressures affect experience of school is difficult to determine – different young people will respond differently to the stresses in their lives and the effect of these factors will vary. It is important to understand the various factors affecting student's lives as they can provide insight into the conflict and difficulty they experience in school. Only when the nature of the difficulty is understood can steps be taken to reduce it.

7

School Work, Educational Provision and Engagement

In previous chapters, we learned about how the interviewees perceive themselves as having low status within the school hierarchy in relation to other students and, especially, to teachers. This chapter considers the interviewees' perceptions of school work, educational provision and their own ability. The interviewees have a unique position and point of view as excluded students. They have been in both mainstream schools and alternative provision Centres and have all experienced upheaval in their educational careers, which may well influence their thoughts about education. We can learn much from their perceptions of the worth of education generally and about provision in mainstream school and the Centres specifically, since they are well placed to make useful comparisons. The chapter ends with the interviewees' perceptions of their own ability and degree of engagement in school and notes how these differ. We see again that 'excluded students' cannot be regarded as one homogeneous group.

The interviewees' standpoints

These students make little distinction between education and school work and seldom speak about the intrinsic value of learning, dwelling rather on work which is done in school and which has a practical use in their lives or which they see as instrumental in helping them to achieve their goals. So when the young people in the sample say that 'education' is important, they generally mean schoolwork, especially that which they see as leading to accreditation. Their perceptions of the purpose of schoolwork are discussed in some detail.

Also relevant is the interesting educational position the interviewees are in, and which colours their perceptions. All have received both mainstream school and small Centre educational provision. Their opinions about the importance of education and reports about their approach to schoolwork may not be the same at the time of interview as it was when they were in school.

One third of the sample specifically mentioned that their view on the importance of education and their approach to schoolwork had changed at some point in their school career – for various reasons. Some young people had a sense that concern for school and schoolwork was something that came with maturity – as one reached the final years of school the importance of working increased.

> Leon: Before that I didn't care about work and that. I just wanted to have my fun. Because I was told by the older pupils that first year and second year you can have your total fun but third and fourth and fifth year you work. That's what I was told, so I took it.

> Lorraine: I was younger then, I didn't really see the point in things, I just thought, 'Oh God'...

For other students the fact that they were approaching the end of their school career and facing the next, often unknown, step was enough to motivate them to engage in their schoolwork.

> Jon: It's just something that happened ...so nothing really mattered to me then. ... But if I got suspended now, it would bother me, 'cause like, I need all the time I can get.

> Eva: So, would you say that your...sounds like you're saying that your attitude has sort of changed?

> Jon: Changed, yeah. I'm going to come to the end of school.

> Shelly: I think it's important, like, if you wanna get a good job or something or you wanna get into college and that. But when I was in my old school, I just thought, 'Yeah', I thought, 'Not worth it' and that. But now, like, I've come here and I've realised that I haven't got that long at school. That's why I want to do well and that.

Increased motivation in the final year of school is not unique to excluded students. Day (1996) found that the vast majority of year 11s reported increasing their effort for GCSE examinations, believing them to be connected with their future success.

Permanent exclusion itself had an impact. There was a wide range of responses to exclusion, ranging from deep regret to relief to indifference.
Some who felt regretful cited their exclusion as the catalyst for a change
of attitude. Nowhere is this more clearly illustrated than with Joshua.

Joshua: When I got expelled, the day that I got expelled I just
remembered because my teacher said to me what do I want
to be when I leave school and I told him that I want to be a
computer programmer.

Eva: Right.

Joshua: And he said, 'How do you intend to do that if you leave here?',
and I says, 'I don't know'. He goes, 'Well you better start
thinking 'cause you're being expelled'. So, um ... that's when
it all changed, I went home and I just thought about it. And I
just changed. I just got on with my work. When I was expelled,
I didn't go to school for about two months, so I used to go to
the library just get loads of books, I just used to read and do
loads of Maths so I didn't fall behind or anything and just do
loads of work then I got into this school [Centre] and I just try
my hardest.

Thus the standpoint from which the young people speak at the time of
their interview may be very different to how they saw matters during
their time at school. We should not lose sight of this while making sense
of the next significant revelation in the young people's accounts: their
common belief in the value of 'education'.

Perceptions of the worth of education

An overwhelmingly consistent view was evident among the interviewees
– that education is of value and academic success desirable. Only four
stated explicitly or implied that schoolwork was of no use to them.

Tuscar: ... Like the same as all the other schools and that, where they
says they're doing all your writing and reading and that, and
English and science, writing it out and that, um, just basic
waste.

This small minority reported education to be 'a waste of time'. Others
expressed a certain ambivalence towards schoolwork, usually by saying
it was good to 'avoid' or 'get out of' work. It is surprising, however, that

so few of the sample expressed such attitudes, considering that all had had such negative experiences in school. Instead, interviewees kept declaring their belief in the importance of school work. How often they did so varied, but their reasons were relatively consistent. Although a few young people mentioned that they did the work to avoid boredom or to please their parents, the vast majority clearly linked work done in school to their employment prospects.

Some of the interviewees mentioned the importance of education for general skill acquisition which would help them in their future lives.

> Eva: I mean how important is it to you, to be in school?
>
> Richard: Very important. I, just, it's not important for when I leave school, 'cause when I leave school I wanna become a DJ and, like, school don't teach ya things to do with DJ. But they teach ya how to handle money and you know English is like, you still need, so that when you go over...like languages as well... when you go to other countries.

Others cited the importance of school in order to gain qualifications.

> Eva: Right. Would you say that you....how do you feel about being here [Centre]?
>
> Neil: Uh. Don't really mind. As long as I get a few GCSEs, I don't really mind where
>
> Eva: Right. Do you have any thoughts on what you'd like to do in the future?
>
> Neil: Yeah. I wanted...I'm not sure which college at the moment, but I want to do Media Studies, GNVQ.
>
> Michael: ... I weren't fussed. They said to me that you've missed, you've had too much time out of school, and you need to catch up on your work, and I go, 'Oh alright then. Put it this way, I want to do my GCSE's so whatever you can do, just do for me'.
>
> Eva: Yeah.
>
> Michael: So I got put in here.

Of course, for most, qualifications are linked to future placements in college, on apprenticeships or in jobs.

> Eva: Good, can you tell me more about how GCSE's help you get a good job? You said you have to do GCSE's to get a good job.

Yaz: Well not a wicked job but, better job than what I'd get if I didn't have GCSE's.

Eva: Really, so how's that work, the GCSE bit, do employers look at your exam results, or how...?

Yaz: Yeah 'cause when you fill in your um, application form, well if you've put no GCSE's then it makes you like a right idiot.

Eva: Right, right, so employers will look at that, and think, oh yeah, she's done a couple of exams, and they'll, they'll take you on?

Yaz: Yeah.

Jade: Just get on with your business in here. That's what I do, just get on with what I come to do to get a grade then go.

Eva: Yeah, I was going to ask you, you know what are the most important reasons for you for coming here?

Jade: Get my grades, that's it.

Eva: Yeah.

Jade: Get my grades and go to college.

Eva: Right, I wonder what's important for you, for getting on with your coursework?

Tariq: 'Cause if not then I can't do any of my GCSE's unless I do that.

Eva: Okay, so what would happen if you couldn't do your GCSE's?

Tariq: Wouldn't get a job or nothing.

Many others simply connect education generally to jobs.

Jon: Well, gotta try and get as much work as I've done, to get best grade I can, and get a good job. Hopefully.

Eva: But, but for you, how important is learning?

Lorraine: It is important in a way, because I do want a nice life when I'm older, I want a nice settled job, and everything like that. But sometimes I just, sometimes I don't wanna come here, but I just think, what am I gonna get out of it, if I don't come here?

These views hardly indicate an anti-education or even anti-school sentiment that might be expected from students permanently excluded from school. It might be natural for them to reject the system and institution that had rejected them. Most interviewees described antagonistic relations with some or most of their teachers and this is clearly one characteristic of anti-school groups. The interviewees expressed belief in the value of education and their desire to succeed seems at odds with such expectations. That so many of them appear to value education and qualifications and perceive them as intrinsically and positively linked to their futures is fascinating.

Linking this valuing of education to the change of heart many of them report between their time at school and in the Centre is revealing. This change can not be attributed entirely to the interviewees' position in their educational career or the shock of permanent exclusion itself. Day (1996) reports that although national assessment motivates some students, those who think they have little chance of success are distanced further from learning (p.169). Many but not all of the students in the present study experienced little academic success in school, and yet they describe themselves as more engaged than ever in their study in the Centres. This suggests that there is something about the way in which the Centres operate that motivates the young people to work and feel positively about their potential for academic and career success.

Perceptions of provision: Schools and Centres

Nineteen of the interviewees stated explicitly that they received more help at the Centre or were able to do more work there, or both. The following comments are indicative of these interviewees' feelings about the educational provision they received in the Centres.

Kirsty: Yeah. I've done more since I've been here, than I done in my school life.

Jon: I've learnt quite a lot here. I think I've learnt more here than I ever have, being at school.

Eva: You've learned more?

Jon: Truthfully, I mean I could never draw anything, and [my] Art work is just brilliant. I mean like Maths work, English work, and things like that. I think I've learnt more here, in the time I've been here, which is about 10 months or something, than I ever had in school.

Eva: Wow.

Jon: It's 'cause you get on more, it's a better environment. There's only a couple odd to a class, you call the teachers by their first name, we're like friends, rather than teachers. And you just get on better, so you do your work better.

Tuscar:	Like, it's littler, littler classes, so.
Eva:	Oh yeah.
Tuscar:	Don't have to sit down for ages waiting for a teacher.
Eva:	Oh okay. So having somebody being able to answer your questions right away, is important?
Tuscar:	Yeah. And like at school, the teachers would just ignore me anyway, so.

Comments such as these were abundant. The central is clear: smaller class sizes and positive relationships with teachers result in more work being done – and that 'doing work' is valued by the interviewees. It is no surprise, then, that 'not getting work done' in school is viewed as a problem. The interviewees' accounts of their educational provision in school demonstrated not only the importance of doing work but also their recognition of the status of this work. Woods (1990) comments that students are acutely aware of the status of work and that only work 'that counts' will be regarded as worthwhile by students (p.158). The following comments of some young people, both positive and negative, on their curriculum at school demonstrates their feelings related to the work in which they were asked to engage.

Eva:	Yeah? Is there any difference between the work at school and the work here?
Nathan:	Nah. Except that at that school they used to give you these mad sheets and you had to draw jewellery and stuff and it was crap.
Eva:	Oh really.
Nathan:	You know when the teacher's away and you've got a substitute teacher? I drew designs for pizza boxes everyday.
Carl:	Yeah, or like in Maths lesson when we kept on talking to the teacher all the time.
Eva:	Yeah.
Carl:	If it's like a lesson like that, then we just go to the park 'cause it's a waste of time going 'cause we're not gonna do no work see.
Nahim:	Yeah, the form teacher, she used to, she used to teach us English, but I think you have to know about banks and everything.
Eva:	Oh yeah.

Nahim: Like we used to have like, um, what is it called? There's a free period like, but.

Eva: Right.

Nahim: The form teacher takes it, and you talk about whatever you want. She used to tell us about what we have to know about, you know, compensation and that.

These comments show the importance to the young people of work that has meaning. Work is judged to have meaning because is seen as practical and relevant to the interviewees' lives or because it has the meaning imposed by the system: it is coursework and it 'counts'. The absence of meaningful work is the source of discontent and can be the impetus for truancy – as in Carl's case.

Behaviour in, and attitude towards, lessons is determined by two factors (Woods, 1990): work that counts and the teacher's attitude and approach. The interviewees' perceptions of the effort teachers put into classes and the expectations of the teachers and the school strongly influences their attitude towards schoolwork.

Shelly: Well, uh, with...when I was there...when I was like having geography and that, like I didn't like the teacher and the lesson and that 'cause he used to just give you work and say 'Get on with it'. He didn't used to explain and that. And I didn't know what to do...

Carl: But like in a top set the teacher will want you to do something.

Eva: Be expecting more of you?

Carl: Yeah, but you um, still could like talk and that, but used to make you work as well.

Eva: Oh I see, where, in lower sets, you talk and don't have to do work?

Carl: Yeah.

Eva: Right.

Carl: And in lower sets as well, the work would be easy. They don't bother with you.

Both Nahim and Carl experienced changing sets during their school career and their remarks about this provide valuable insight into students' perceptions of the differentiated expectations of teachers, as we shall see. The student's relationship with the teacher can often be the key influence on their approach to lessons.

Michael: And she can't understand why I'm not doing the work, but really she knows, she knows. She's left now ... but end of the day man, she didn't like me at all, I didn't like her.

Eva: Right. And so because of how you've been treated, that means, you now don't want to do the work in her subjects?

Michael: I would do the work, but not with her, because if somebody brought another teacher in, I would do the work.

Michael's words highlight the way that, whether students are generally disposed positively or negatively towards school and schoolwork, they will behave differently from one lesson to another. Woods (1990) observes that the student's working pattern may vary according to various features of the lesson such as the teacher, subject and time of day (p.285). This helps explain the variety of approaches the young people in this study described in relation to their lessons, and particularly the quite different responses described by Shelly, Carl and Michael to one lesson as compared to another.

The factors that influenced the interviewees' attitude towards schoolwork – the status of the work, the relationship with the teacher and their enjoyment of the subject – were the same in school and the Centre. Yet the way young people positioned themselves *vis-à-vis* school work was totally different in the two institutions. In the Centres young people described themselves as working hard, achieving academically and valuing school work. Only a small handful described their relationship to school work in school in a similar manner. Generally, the young people in the sample appeared to be students who experienced a distinct lack of success in school, yet in the Centre perceived themselves to be successful or potentially successful in school. The shift in perception suggests that the factors corresponding to lack of success in school lay not exclusively with the young people but also with features related to the structure, organisation and operation of the school. That the Centres manage to change the attitudes and self-perceptions of these students is impressive.

Throughout the 1980s there was much research undertaken linking various school factors to levels of disruption in schools (Rutter *et al.*, 1979; Reynolds, 1982; Reid, 1986; McManus, 1987). This work emphasised the importance of school 'ethos' or 'culture' on the behaviour of students – the students' participation in school life, the psychological environment of the classroom, teacher expectations and the balance between rewards and punishments (see Reynolds,1982). A focus on ethos explains the interviewees' shifts of opinion between school and Centre. As they themselves say, small class sizes, quality relationships and a focus on exam-related work contribute to the positive atmosphere of the Centres and their own success studying in them.

The adequacy of Centre provision is much discussed (see *Guardian*, 26-11-96; Lovey *et al.*, 1993; OFSTED, 1993) and Centres are criticised for offering students only part-time education, due to their lack of funding. The students expressed mixed reactions: some felt that shorter hours were better because it suited their learning style, allowed them to do other things in the day, and discouraged them from truanting, while others felt that they would prefer longer hours and a greater range of subjects. It is interesting that, although the hours spent in the Centre were fewer than in school, many of the young people felt they achieved far more. The vast majority of the interviewees stated that they preferred BSS Centre provision over school (only six stated that they would prefer school). The following comment helps to shed light on this preference.

> Nathan: I think that, uh, schools can offer you better stuff but they don't give it to the people that come here. If we was in proper school, we wouldn't be offered it, so we're not losing out
>
> Eva: OK. And what would you say are the reasons that you wouldn't be offered it?
>
> Nathan: I can't be trusted. I don't think most of the people here would either. You get the people, the quiet ones, they'd be trusted.
>
> Eva: Yeah.
>
> Nathan: But not people like Edward and all that.

Schools are perceived to be *capable* of providing better provision, but failing to offer it to lower-status students. The Centres, with their limited curriculum, are deemed preferable because they offer these students at least some opportunity to achieve.

The views of the young people in the study have so far been discussed as if they were relatively unified – and there is indeed a large degree of consistency in their views on the importance, purpose and instrumental value of education and of Centre provision. But there are striking and significant differences in how interviewees regard schoolwork and their ability and the degree to which they demonstrate engagement with the school system.

Perceptions of ability

The 1996 OFSTED study of exclusion found that very few of the students were of 'above-average' ability but were evenly divided between 'average' and 'below-average' ability. I am less concerned with the interviewees' ability than with their own perceptions of that ability. This proved to be difficult to uncover. Many of them were ambiguous about their position or did not mention it but others did discuss their perceptions of themselves as learners. In light of these descriptions, the students can be placed loosely into three groups: those who perceive themselves to be of low ability or experiencing difficulty academically, those who perceive themselves to be of higher ability in higher streams and those who felt their performance or set-placement did not match their ability.

Difficulty with schoolwork, or self-perceived low ability emerged in various ways. Most forthright were Charles and Tuscar, who reported being in the bottom set, whereas Anthony is more oblique:

Anthony: 'Cause I'm not, I'm not the smartest person in the year, I'm not the dumbest either.

Eva: Mm mm.

Anthony: I do have difficulty, quite slow in work.

So Anthony, too, sees his ability as low. So does Sandra, who relates ability specifically to literacy. She experienced extreme difficulty in reading and this has affected her aspirations for the future.

Sandra: Because I'm not good at reading or nothing, I wanted to be a vet, but, I don't know what to put down, or nothing. And 'cause I can't exactly read the labels and the things and everything, 'cause I don't really read at all.

Eva: Right.

Sandra: So I would be um, you know, I'd make a fool of myself if I try and work there.

Eva: Right. And did you come to that, you know that conclusion by, by yourself, or did...

Sandra: Yeah. I could tell, by you know, my work and everything. I can't read words and that, and I found out, so, it isn't worth me trying my luck really, 'cause I can't do it.

Although Sandra is referring to the world of work, her difficulty in reading would obviously affect most aspects of her school life. Dana, Jade, Tonya, Kirsty, Shelly and Michael all describe having some difficulty in school but do not say which set they were in at the time, so how their difficulty relates to ability is uncertain. For at least some of them missing school and then needing to catch up was the problem. What matters here is that all these students perceived themselves as experiencing some difficulty in lessons.

Another group described themselves as quite able. Damien reports that he was in the first, second or third set for all his classes, while Tariq says that he found lessons easy. Joshua and Leon have this to say:

> Joshua: Yeah the work was ... like quite easy. I was in one of the top groups. I found the work easy ... and I think that's why I never done the work most of the time because it was too easy.

> Leon: I liked that school a lot because, I had the...if I had never had that [exclusion], everything was going right for me. Perfect. Just messed. Like I was taking the top exams as well, I was taking all of my exams and here [Centre] I had to go a bit down.

High academic ability and top streams are not expected to be characteristic of excluded students, as OFSTED (1996) shows. Joshua identifies being in the wrong stream as a source of concern to him and young people in a third group also claim that their assigned set and their personal performance do not reflect their ability. Nathan describes himself as being in a class of 'the rejects of the year', and yet he says he finds the work easy at both school and the Centre.

> Eva: Oh yeah? How do you find school work?
> Nathan: I think it's easy you know. I'm not trying to sound like...but I do think it's easy.

Nathan made several comments about an unstimulating and unpalatable curriculum. Although he does not say so himself, he probably was not given schoolwork that matched his ability and challenged him. Manny, on the other hand, is clear that he was wrongly assigned to the bottom set.

Manny:	It's boring Miss, I was in the wrong set Miss, I thought I was in the wrong set Miss.
Eva:	Yeah, so how
Manny:	I don't know about the teachers, but I thought I was in the wrong set, I was like in the bottom set Miss.
Eva:	Right.
Manny:	Group five Miss. And they were like doing things that people do in year seven Miss, like easy stuff.
Eva:	Right, what set should you have been in?
Manny:	About set three or set four Miss.
Eva:	Yeah.
Manny:	Set five, the words weren't more than about five letters long Miss, six letters long...

It is possible that these young men were placed in lower sets more because of their behaviour than their ability.

Self-perceptions with regard to their ability varied widely. Interestingly, the majority of the interviewees who considered themselves able were African-Caribbean and Asian. The OFSTED (1996) report suggests that this is part of a national trend:

> The case-histories of most of the Caribbean children differed markedly from those of others studied for this survey...most of them were of average or above average ability but had been assessed by the schools as under-achieving. (OFSTED, 1996, p.11)

The racialised nature of exclusion is usually related to the dispropor-tionate number of African-Caribbean and growing number of Asian males excluded from school (*TES*, 5-3-99, *Guardian*, 11-10-96) but this study also reveals differences in the abilities of the white and ethnic minority students who are excluded. Linked to variation in ability is variation in the extent to which young people are 'engaged' in the educa-tional system and this is now discussed.

Engagement

Elliott (1998) and Wallace (1996), among others, use 'engagement' to indicate whether students are engaged in school work and learning but here 'engagement' refers to the students' understanding of and active involvement in the wider education system. One student, for example, who aims to take a college GNVQ understands that he needs four passes to get into the programme and may, if he achieves high grades, be eligible for the Advanced GNVQ. The students in this study rarely show that they have specific, detailed information about the education system – in this case the transition between school and college. Many discuss school work in vague terms, simply equating doing well with getting a job. Others identify the importance of GCSEs, but do not discuss and seem unclear about how GCSEs will translate into work or college placements. It is significant that the student who did make the connection is the one member of the sample who can be considered middle-class, and was excluded from a fee-paying boarding school. The others demonstrate a much less detailed grasp of how the educational system operates, although several show that they understand some of its features.

> Yvonne: Well, I want to do one year ... doing an NVQ, one year doing a BTEC at the College of Food. 'Cause I want to become a Nursery Nurse, and I'll be qualified for that by the time I'm 18. Want to keep at that for a couple of years. And I want to get more qualifications and [be] able to be a primary school teacher. And then like, when I'm, later on like when I'm 30, late 30s, like 39/40, I want to become a midwife. I want to keep my options open, don't want to stick to one thing, but it's all to do with kids and babies.

Here Yvonne demonstrates her understanding of the formal system of education and accreditation and also her vested interest in it. Other interviewees also indicate a vested interest in the system. Leon is concerned that his exclusion meant that 'I missed a lot. Missed my mock exams as well', and he tells me that between exclusion and placement at a Centre...

> Leon: I studied a lot. My dad bought me the GCSE revision books and I just studied a lot.

Both Manny and Joshua describe their frustration at not being moved up in sets when they believed themselves capable.

> Joshua: Yeah, I found the work too easy, I was not in the top group, but about two groups before the top and I found the work to easy and they could have easily transferred me to a higher group.

Eva: Right.

Joshua: Where I could have found the work harder or something. But
           they never done nothing about it. I was just getting bored in
           my lessons

Eva: Mmm and did you say that you had said something to them
           about how it was too easy?

Joshua: Yeah I told the teacher that it was too easy, and they said that
           they had noticed that through my exams and everything,
           because I used to get top marks in my exams and they told
           me that they noticed. And they were saying that they were
           going to do something about it but they never, it just carried
           on.

Manny: I did Miss, and he goes that he knows when it is time for me
           to go up ...

Eva: And he thought that that was the right decision?

Manny: Yeah Miss, he goes that 'I know when it will be time for you to
           move up', Miss.

These two young men and Leon were the only students to express concern about being in the Centre and the effect it might have on their future. Although Leon felt that he had achieved more work in the Centre, especially in Maths, he was concerned about the number and level of difficulty of the subjects he was studying: 'I'm taking fewer and the standard is down as well'. And Joshua regrets completing his education in a BSS Centre.

Joshua: I wish I would have stayed in secondary school, if I would
           have stayed in secondary school I could have done all my
           GCSE's, because I'm only doing a couple here.

Joshua: It makes me feel different to every one else in proper school.
           I have to be put with different, lesser class. Some people are
           like, they can't...I don't know how to say it. They're, like, they
           aren't as forward as everyone else. You feel different, you feel
           like what am I doing here like, I shouldn't be here I should be
           in a proper school. But I know that ain't going to happen so I
           just try. It's different because there's only two years, year ten
           and year eleven, different quite a lot. You don't like change
           lessons, you are only in school half the day. Different.

Eva: So some people here aren't as forward?

Joshua: No they're not backwards or anything, they are just like ... like they have been bullied and like ... I don't know they don't seem as, I don't know if they are or not but they don't seem as brainy, like I find some people compared to me not as brainy as me.

Joshua recognises the negative academic implications of his exclusion and subsequent placement in a BSS Centre and he also identifies problematic aspects of Centre life relating to his social relations. He clearly identifies himself as different and separate to the other young people attending the Centre and does not enjoy the feeling of being different.

Manny also feels at a disadvantage in the Centre. For one thing, he recognises that he is missing out on the quantity and range of education he would receive at school, 'Science you have six lessons of it [in school] and here you have one lesson. English you used to have three or four and here you have two, and History and things like that, Miss. You don't do PE or anything like that, Miss'. He also says that he misses being in the company of other Asian students.

Manny: ... nothing wrong with the people here, Miss, just like I was more used to a lot more Asian people at school like that, Miss.

Eva: Right, how do you feel about there being more, when there's more Asians?

Manny: It's just like you can be more free with them ain't it, Miss?

In addition, Manny recognises the inferior status held by BSS Centres in the wider education system and the incongruity of his being at one when his family's educational expectations are so different.

Manny: ...I started off in school and ended up somewhere like here, Miss, and he's [father] a bit disappointed, Miss.

Eva: Right, how do you feel about that?

Manny: Let him down, Miss. My brother, Miss, my older one, he goes to Uni, Miss.

Eva: Oh does he?

Manny: Aston University.

Eva: Oh does he.

Manny: Yeah, Miss. Everyone else is alright in my family apart from me, Miss.

The reality is that attending a BSS Centre has lower status than attending school. Students do not have the opportunity to take such a wide a range of exams and furthermore, employers are likely to question why a candidate for a job was in need of Behavioural Support Services and may be reluctant to employ someone who has attended a Centre. The majority of the interviewees either do not recognise this or are not concerned. They feel that the Centre meets their needs by providing an atmosphere in which they can learn and gain qualifications that will help them in their future. It is significant, then, that these few young people recognise the inferior status of the Centres. Somehow they seem more conversant with how the educational system operates. By possessing this knowledge and by perceiving themselves as able, they set themselves apart. Whereas Neil, Joshua, Leon, Manny and Yvonne describe some behaviour in school that might be expected from 'disaffected' young people, they seem to be much more engaged in their academic careers than the other interviewees. Also significant is the fact that four of these five young people are from ethnic minority groups, a vastly disproportionate number given the sample.

In 1977, Paul Willis published his study of working-class lads and their transition from school to the workplace. The lads show no interest in school and seem resigned to work which would be distant, meaningless and manual, whereas the excluded students, although sharing some of the lads' opinions, are engaged in their schoolwork and aspire to jobs that have meaning and will bring them satisfaction. This may partly reflect the drop over the last twenty years in manual jobs but it may also indicate a distinct difference between the aspirations of working class young people from ethnic minority groups and those of their white counterparts. This is too small a group upon which to theorise about the nature of working-class ethnic minority culture and school identity. But it does have significance: first, they show that the educational experience of 'excluded students' is not universal and, second, some of this variation may be related to ethnicity.

Conclusion

Two features of the interviewees' attitudes towards and experiences of school work are significant. The first is their expressed desire to learn and succeed coupled with the general belief that it was possible to do so in BSS Centres. This lends support to research that attributes much of the causes of disruptive behaviour to the structure of school. Since young people who reported that they did not succeed in school perceived themselves as doing so in Centres, it seems useful to ask what schools can learn from Centres about managing difficult behaviour and promoting achievement. In particular, what are the structural and organisational features of the Centres that promote such positive relations between students and teachers and to what extent, if any, could these be incorporated into schools? These questions will be explored in the next chapter.

The second important finding in this chapter is that a few interviewees report a different educational experience from the majority. Whereas most, although valuing 'education' in general terms, seemed somewhat disengaged from the educational system, these few seemed more engaged in the system and to have more at stake within it. They are the young people who seem unlikely candidates for exclusion and yet they have been permanently excluded. The fact that four of the five are from ethnic minority groups hints at a number of larger issues such as the racialised nature of exclusion and also considerations about the nature of working-class ethnic minority culture. The sub-sample here is far too small to allow conclusions to be drawn but it does highlight an important area for further research. What this small group shows us is that the experiences of excluded students differ in ways that are important and need to be understood.

8

Schools and Centres as Learning Environments

Thus far, the young people's experience of school has been broken down into individual components, which are then explored in detail. This chapter looks at the 'big picture' of the educational experience. The school and the Centre are compared as learning environments.

The purpose is to look at educational institutions as social systems and examine the social forces that shape young people's educational experiences. Because these young people have had the unique educational experience of attending both mainstream school and alternative education Centres, their accounts allow for a powerful comparison.

Schools as a social system

The young people in this study have had a predominantly negative experience in the social system of school. They describe themselves as being unable to negotiate their way successfully through this system. A key concept in explaining this experience of school is that of borders, borders which are seen to be restrictive or even prohibitive. They act as barriers to achieving a positive experience of school. The more tightly an experience is bound by borders, the less likely it is to be positive. The two types of borders that shape the experience of the young people in this study are those imposed by external factors and those that are self-constructed. Structural features of the social system impose restrictions on individuals' experiences, and individuals also impose restrictions on themselves.

Imposed borders take on a number of forms. Phelan *et al.* (1993) identify several imposed borders that impact on the students in their study: sociocultural, socio-economic, linguistic and gender. These borders exist when the knowledge and skill set of one group is valued over that of another (p.53). At schools this tends to mean that the 'culture' of the student is not recognised as valuable in school. The knowledge held by 'the school' and its agents is seen to be legitimate or 'right', while the knowledge that students bring with them from home and personal experience is disregarded. If this is the situation, then who or what forces determine the value of knowledge held in different 'cultures'? This 'differential value' must be determined against certain criteria and by particular individuals or groups. In school, the criteria for determining the worth of individuals are set by the formal educational system – the teaching staff and the system within which they operate. The accepted norms and values of the formal system constitute the 'dominant discourse' and this determines what knowledge, skills and even individuals are valuable. The present system thus constructs restrictive borders for those individuals and groups whose knowledge and skills are deemed less valuable.

We have seen that a hierarchy of worth exists in school that is completely school- and teacher-defined. What is valued is a particular type of behaviour and academic performance and the students perceived as more successful or as possessing more of the valued knowledge and skills are afforded higher status. The young people in the study recognise that some of their peers in school are more highly valued than others, and they clearly recognise the qualities for which they are valued: those who 'can do the work', are 'the brightest in the class' or 'the quiet ones' are those whom the teachers value most highly. From interviewees' accounts we see that this status is perceived to be rewarded with better quality teaching, more positive relations with teachers and favourably-biased disciplinary action.

One of the most significant ways in which the dominant discourse exercises and maintains its power is by determining the legitimate 'voice' within the system. Whose voice 'counts' at school? Who gets to be heard? One of the common complaints of the young people is that they were not listened to. The interviewees were talking about specific patterns of interactions between themselves and teachers but the issue runs deeper than the specific behaviours of individuals. The interviewees' perception that they are not listened to can be seen as a manifestation of how borders operate to deem certain voices legitimate while others are not. When two actors within a social system speak, who is heard? Whose views are acted upon and whose interests set the agenda? The dominant discourse that prevails within a social system determines which views and interests are the legitimate ones within it. In school, the formal hierarchy mediates who is heard. As Giroux (1989) observes,

> In many cases, schools do not allow students from subordinate groups to authenticate their problems and lived experiences through their own individual and collective voices... the dominant school culture generally represents and legitimates the privileged voices of the white middle and upper classes. (p.143).

In this study, the students were almost all working-class. Teachers tend to be middle-class so it is not surprising that the most obvious differential in the status of views exists between teachers and students. Between these two sets of actors, teachers are clearly seen to have the voice that 'counts' in school and their actions and decisions to hold greater weight than any student's.

The teacher's knowledge, views and perceptions are held more representative of the 'truth' than the students'. As Tonya says:

> Tonya: ...like the teacher will say something wrong to ya....so you go to report it, but before you report it, that teacher's already gone down to the headmaster and said her side of the story already, you know. And then when we get there, or when whoever gets there, [they say] 'Oh, well we've heard the story. You're not telling the truth'...

The students in this study have a voice that is seldom heard and almost never recognised as significant. The various borders that are imposed upon their world prevent their being heard and their views valued. Indeed, their 'truth' seems not to count.

Students recognise this systemic bias being directed against them but do not identify it as such. Although they do not talk about borders restricting their potential, they do recognise that differential value is assigned to students and that that assigned to them is disadvantageous within the social system of school. They see themselves as possessing little status in the school hierarchy and often feel as if their views and needs, whether pastoral or academic, are disregarded. Some wished that they had seen more teacher intervention into their conflicts with other students. Others felt that they were not offered schoolwork appropriate to their ability, even when they complained. There may be many reasons why these students' needs were not met, not least the prevailing teaching conditions such as large class sizes and pressures of examination targets. The study does not criticise the failure of individual teachers but aims rather to highlight the restrictive aspects of the system in which students and teachers have to operate.

In addition to these imposed borders, and often in response to them, the young people themselves create borders that limit their chances of enjoying a positive experience of school. Phelan *et al.* (1994) observe that 'psychosocial borders are constructed when children experience anxiety, depression, apprehension or fear at a level that disrupts or hinders their ability to focus on classroom tasks, or blocks their ability to establish relationships with teachers or peers in school environments' (1993, p.57). They point out that psychosocial borders can be constructed either in response to imposed borders or as a reaction to stress in other aspects of their lives, such as at home. This study revealed self-constructed borders of both kinds. We have heard accounts by young people who attribute the difficulties they encounter at school to difficulties at home, such as the illness or absence of a parent. One interviewee described coming to school 'with a chip on me shoulder', rooted in the absence of his father from home, and felt that this 'chip' made him vulnerable to his peers and prone to conflict with them. Young people bring to school their knowledge, skills and experience. Some experiences, and the resulting beliefs and attitudes, may make it difficult for them to enter smoothly into the culture of the school and this can lead to conflict.

The borders students construct in response to those they find imposed are more subtle. They were perhaps most evident in their accounts of the low expectations of teachers and their counter-response. Several commented on some teachers' lack of effort on behalf of lower status classes and how the students responded by 'messing about'. The 'messing about' is perceived to perpetuate the teacher's view that the class was unworthy of 'real' teaching, so limiting the young people's educational experience.

Borders like these are constructed in opposition to a dominant discourse that does not value the young people. Tony Sewell (1997) discusses the various ways that African-Caribbean boys construct school identities in opposition to a system that disadvantages them. He regarded many of them as conformist, since they accepted both the goals and means of the education system. Other boys positioned themselves differently, some accepting the goals of school but not the means and others rejecting both the goals and the means. These positions can be understood in terms of borders as discussed in the present book.

Borders differentiate knowledge and skill sets according to their 'value', which is determined by the dominant discourse. In self-constructed borders, however, 'value' is re-assessed by individuals. By rejecting the goals and/or means of schooling, Sewell's students show that they do not value the knowledge and skill sets presented by the dominant discourse. Borders of this nature serve two opposing functions: to protect and to exclude. Sewell comments on the positioning of the Posse, a small rebellious group: 'the Posse were creating a sub-culture of resistance to schooling which was essentially concerned with collective protection and survival' (p.116). Although this position served to protect these young people, it also disadvantaged them. Poor relations with teachers and other educational agents restricts or prevents access to the information and guidance that facilitate future social and economic success (see Stanton-Salazar (1997) for full discussion).

The concept of protective borders is useful in the present study. These borders could help students navigate their way through the social system of school without experiencing the difficulties the young people in this study describe. Some of Sewell's students rejected the means and/or goals of the school, and yet managed to stay out of trouble. When Sewell asks David whether he had been excluded by the former headmaster. He replies, '*No, he couldn't because I'm a bad boy. I do bad things, but I never get caught*' (p.105). Another boy, Joseph, asked if he had ever been excluded, said that he had not, explaining, '*Because I'm not that rude around teachers*' (p.112). These students largely rejected the set of beliefs and behaviours advocated and valued by the school. They possessed an alternative set of skills, however, that allowed them to manoeuvre their way through school with less difficulty and confrontation than the students in the present study.

Why should the excluded students have experienced difficulty in school, with such serious consequences, when other young people operating within similar structural conditions did not? Have they failed to develop the skills to protect themselves from a social system biased against them? Have they not learned the responses or behaviour deemed appropriate within the dominant discourse? Or are they unable to filter the negative experiences, such as humiliating teacher comments, in a way considered suitable by the institution – something that other young people may be able to do? A lack of emotional awareness and/or ability to manage emotions may set up borders that restrict a young person's potential for developing a positive school identity and, consequently, a positive experience of school.

Self-constructed borders are one way for individuals to shape and influence their experience. They might be a response to structural restrictions in school or be due to the student's personality. Few of the interviewees exhibit a skill set that enables them to stay 'out of trouble' with teachers – which may help to explain why they were the ones who experienced difficulty and were excluded from school while others in a similar situation were not. It is important to understand the role of the individual in creating difficult situations but it is equally important to recognise that often when the structural conditions change, so does the individual's behaviour, perception and experience.

A different experience: the Centres

The interviewees' experiences in school were tightly constrained by borders, whether imposed or self-constructed. Within the dominant school discourse, their views did not count and their voices were not heard. This was seen most clearly through the interviewees' accounts of not being listened to, particularly when they were reporting on disruptive incidents. A common complaint was that teachers wouldn't listen to the student's 'side of the story'. The implication is that the students' words were not only not *heard* but also not *valued*. The interviewees' sense of being under-valued was further derived from their academic experiences. Many described a curriculum and teaching style that they thought demonstrated a lack of effort by the teachers and little genuine concern for the students' learning.

The experience described in the BSS Centres, however, was almost wholly positive. Only six of the interviewees stated that they would prefer to be in school, primarily because they believed the provision to be superior there, and even these all describe positive educational experiences in the Centre. The components of the Centre experience that the interviewees highlight are:

- good relationships with teachers

- small classes

- appropriate work and the help they deem necessary to complete it

- more 'relaxed' and 'personal' discipline

- positive or at least neutral relations with peers

The last factor showed the least drastic change between school and the Centres. A few interviewees reported conflict and fighting during their time at the Centre just as they had at school. What was different in the Centres, however, was the absence of the pervasive sense of malice amongst peers that seemed to characterise the interviewees' social world in mainstream school.

In an earlier chapter, we saw that many of the interviewees perceived themselves to be working harder and achieving more in the Centres than at school and such self-perceptions are likely to reflect a more positive sense of self and a greater belief in personal ability. Several interviewees reported a greater sense of control over their behaviour and this too is likely to be linked to a more positive self-perception. Some interviewees mentioned their parents' positive view of the Centre and their children's achievements there. We also saw a change in the interviewees' attitude towards schoolwork. From their position in the Centre, most reported valuing schoolwork, which had not been their view while at school. It is likely that this change was due to their positive experience in the Centre. Linked to this shift in attitude is the change in aspiration towards work shown by a few students, such as Nathan, who says '...before I came here, my dad's cousin wanted me to work with him just doing the cleaning and that – cleaning flats and I would have ended up in a dead-end job doing that. But I came here, so I want to do horticulture and that again'.

So what was it about the Centre that so positively affected these young people, particularly in contrast with their largely negative experience of school? We have seen that the interviewees in this study are low-status students in mainstream school, lacking institutional power. They do not feel this way in the Centres. However, it is not that they have moved up the social hierarchy in the Centres but that the very shape of the social system is different. First, and most notably, the hierarchical distance between teachers and students seems greatly reduced. Although the teachers still hold a greater share of responsibility and institutional power, interactions with students seem qualitatively different. It is from the young people's descriptions of their relationships with Centre teachers that the notion of adult-like interactions arose. Being spoken to like 'adults' or 'friends' was an often-cited benefit of attending the Centre, and the power differential is not felt the same way as at school. The interviewees did not describe the teacher-student relationship in the Centre in terms of an adult-child dichotomy – interactions were described as more balanced. Not that the relationship is essentially even – teachers need to carry more responsibility and have greater decision-making power – but nonetheless, interactions between teachers and student *feel* even to the students.

The second way in which the social system of the Centres differs from that of mainstream school is that there is no sense that the student population is differentially valued. One may argue that this is because the Centres are occupied by students who are all of a similar 'type', but this is not so. The BSS Centres provide education for young people who are permanently excluded from school but also for those who refuse to attend school and who have experienced difficulties at school of a quite different nature. They have most often fled school because of being bullied and rarely have a history of disruption in class. So the absence of a student hierarchy cannot be attributed to a homogeneous student body. More likely the small number of students at a Centre is the significant factor. With fewer students, teachers may have less need to 'sort' students by categorising them into a hierarchy against pre-determined criteria (see Hargreaves, 1967; Becker, 1971 for discussion). Students at the Centre were loosely grouped by ability. Yet, interestingly they made no comment about these groupings either because they were unaware of them or because it seemed not to matter. Further, the interviewees did not express a sense that any particular individual or group was more highly valued than any other. Whether this lack of differentiation is due to the size of the Centre or the approach of the teachers and the institution's ethos is difficult to determine. It is likely that all these characteristics interact and together shape this feature of Centre education.

What is significant is that the nature of the dominant discourse is different in schools and in Centres. Yet the difference is not radical. The Centre is very much part of the formal education system, responsible for teaching the National Curriculum, where possible, and subject to OFSTED inspections. The Centre is an educational institution where decisions about curriculum, organisation, and discipline are still the responsibility of the teaching staff. What is different is the stance of the Centre staff – their general approach to their work, in both formal teaching and informal interactions with students. The feature that appears to be most clearly valued by the students is that the teachers are seen to be caring and committed to helping students achieve. There does not seem to be a sense, as there was in school, that teachers are only interested in helping some students to achieve. This lack of differentiation is perhaps the most positive feature of the social system in the Centres.

The Centre discourse shares features of mainstream school; for example, it does not move away from valuing individual academic achievement but it does rather underplay it. Students are encouraged to achieve as a result of their individual effort and ability but there is far less competition and differentiation. Interestingly, when the interviewees describe their successes, they compare it not to other students but to their own performance when they were at school. It seems that the success of one student is not measured or achieved at the expense of another.

There also seemed to be many different ways in the Centre in which students could perceive themselves as successful. This became most evident at the end-of-year events I attended in two of the Centres. In both cases a presentation was made to every student, summarising her or his achievements in terms of not only academic success but also successful completion of work experience, involvement in a variety of community programmes, and participation in field trips and special challenges (e.g. mountain biking or rock-climbing). In the Centres, there seemed to be a much broader definition of success and what was 'valuable' than in school.

Earlier, we discussed how borders are created when the knowledge and skill sets are assigned differential value by the dominant group and how this disadvantages those outside the group. Although teachers at the Centres still have more power within the social space than students, by broadening the range of the knowledge valued, the Centre staff, as the dominant group, are able to reduce the impact of restrictive borders on their students. One way to broaden the range of knowledge that is to be valued is to acknowledge the knowledge and skills that students possess. Cummins (1994) comments on the need to 'view students as cultural resource persons and to listen to their *self*-expression' (p.322). Although the students do not mention this explicitly, it is implied in their comments about talking to the teachers 'like friends' and being listened to.

Conclusion

So the social system found in Centres shares some features of mainstream school but also has significant differences and engenders very different experiences for its students. The Centres have managed to create a set of learning conditions in which young people whose school experiences were, by all accounts, failures, can engage in learning and succeed. The single most influential feature of this learning environment for the interviewees was the positive relationships with teachers. The core characteristics of these relationships were that teachers communicated caring, treated students respectfully, and provided the resources, guidance, and support they needed to achieve academically. The foundation for these relationships was a more collaborative set of power relations whereby a greater range of knowledge and skills were valued, and thus seen to contribute to the social field. By valuing the skills and abilities students bring to the Centre, the restrictive borders that exist in the educational system are reduced, allowing the individuals a greater opportunity to have a positive educational experience.

9

What Schools Can Do

The accounts of the young people in this study provide us with vital insights into the experience of school and can be the basis for shaping change and improvement. But is it realistic to advocate such changes on the basis of the accounts of thirty-three young people – such a tiny proportion of the 14,500 young people excluded nationally each year (*TES*, 20-2-98)? Excluded students make up only 0.35% of the entire school population (Final Report to the DFE, 1995). So can generalisations be made to the wider school population from the experiences of this one group of young people? The answer is yes – it *is* realistic and generalisations *can* be made.

For one thing, the interviewees' accounts and perceptions of their experience at school mirrored those of other disaffected students in this country and elsewhere (Lloyd-Smith and Davies, 1995). The key themes highlighted in this book are common to a large group of disaffected students. For another, many aspects of their accounts, particularly their views relating to relationships with teachers, reflect the views of mainstream students, as represented in the literature – it isn't simply disaffected young people who want to establish positive, instrumental relationships with teachers (Woods, 1990, Rudduck *et al.*, 1996). Finally, the theoretical concepts used to help explain these interviewees' experiences are widely applicable. The role of borders and discourse in shaping the experience of school helps to explain the experience of not only the young people in this study, but of school students generally. The concept of restrictive and negative borders, seems at first to be most relevant to young people who experience difficulty at school but the absence of such borders helps to explain the engagement and 'success' of other school students. So what can we learn from the experiences of this group of excluded students?

Ultimately, young people should be educated in mainstream school and everything possible should be done to keep them there. Exclusion from school results in considerable upheaval. Students are taken out of the social system to which they are accustomed. For some young people this comes as a relief, but they pay in terms of the time lost – the interviewees report that several weeks or even months passed between their exclusion and access to alternative provision. And this alternative provision can seldom offer the quality facilities and range of subjects available in schools. A limited choice of subjects, and therefore exams, will certainly have an impact on young people's post-16 choices. Being excluded from school and attending a BSS Centre may also affect young people's future by stigmatising them. Consider the following dialogue:

> Eva: ...do think that being excluded has affected your choices for the future?
>
> Manny: Miss I think so Miss, yeah because when you go for a job interview or a placement Miss and they look at your papers Miss it says BSS at the top Miss, Behaviour Supports Service.
>
> Eva: Yeah.
>
> Manny: And they have to think about it when they read that, Miss.
>
> Eva: Right and how do you think it will affect it?
>
> Manny: Yeah Miss because they have two application forms, one from a normal school Miss and the one from the Behavioural Supports Service Miss, they are more likely to pick the one from school...

Manny's perceptions of the views of employers is likely to be accurate in many cases. Moreover, being excluded from school and the troubled events that lead up to it will undoubtedly dent the student's self-esteem.

Simply remaining in mainstream school, however, will not in itself reduce disaffection and ensure positive educational experiences. Indeed, for most of the interviewees, the most positive experience in their educational careers was in the Centres. We can learn from their experience to change matters in the schools. The positive experiences of excluded students in BSS Centres must be used to inform and change mainstream school.

In suggesting how this might be achieved, let us remind ourselves of the factors that have made school life so difficult for these young people. We know that there are a number of factors that shape school experience and have heard in-depth accounts of how interactions with teachers, peers, family members and the legal system impacted on the experience of school. They paint a fairly clear picture.

The young people in the study experienced difficulty in one or more of these areas, although not often in all of them. The experiences combine

---

Figure 9.1: The difficulties experienced by excluded students in school

Individual
• Feel they have little control over their behaviour.

• Many describe themselves as 'easy to wind up' and highly susceptible to peer pressure and antagonism.

Teachers
Relationships with teachers are the most commonly cited source of difficulty. Teacher behaviours deemed problematic:

• not listening to young people's views and experiences of particular events ('their side of the story').

• not intervening to provide pastoral care, particularly in relation to conflict with peers.

• humiliating and/or antagonising students by behaviour such as shouting, insulting, speaking sarcastically, telling them to shut up.

• treating students unequally.

• not providing the help students feel they need to engage in and complete school work.

These behaviours, whether actual or perceived, communicate to students that they are not valued.

Peers
• Concern about being picked on and made fun of. The world of peers is emotionally unsafe.

School Work
Unstimulating and/or irrelevant curriculum:

• because of the lack of effort a teacher puts into a lesson.

• because students are placed in an inappropriate set for their ability.

The message received is that they 'are not worth the effort'.

Factors Outside School
Some young people carry the difficulties they experience outside of school into the school arena, such as:
• family crisis or generally difficult circumstances at home.

• pressure from peers outside school to take part in activities counter to dominant school culture.

• involvement with police and courts.

to provide a clear picture of how we would *not* like school students' educational experience to be. The experience in the Centres, described in earlier chapters, provides us with a more constructive picture – of positive relationships with teachers, minimal disruptive behaviour, the relative absence of malicious peer relations, and the opportunity to engage successfully in schoolwork.

The Centre, as a social system, is not dissimilar to school. Both have teachers, secondary-school aged students, and a range of support staff. The prime 'business' of both is formal education, both are subject to many of the same government and LEA regulations, the teachers share many of the same professional concerns and affiliations and the students largely echo the concerns and difficulties expressed by other young people of a similar age. Yet the interviewees identified distinct differences between the Centres and mainstream school. Some are to do with the structure and organisation of the Centres: very small class sizes, no uniforms, shorter hours of attendance – all features of Centre provision that schools could not replicate. But what counts most to the students are the differences in the interactions between them and the teachers. The relationships young people establish with teachers most significantly affect their school lives. It is here that important lessons can be learned by mainstream schools.

Stanton-Salazar (1997) highlights the significance of positive teacher-student relationships at school to young people's long-term success – since institutional agents are essential for giving them the knowledge, support and access they need to succeed. He also identifies that establishing positive instrumental relationships is problematic for low status youth.

> First, for all children and youths, healthy human development, general well-being, school success, and economic and social integration in society depend upon regular and unobstructed opportunities for constructing instrumental relationships with institutional agents across key social spheres and institutional domains dispersed throughout society (Wynn *et al.*, 1987). Second, for low-status children and youth, the development of supportive relations with institutional agents outside the immediate kinship unit is systematically problematic. (Stanton-Salazar, 1997, p.6)

In the Centres, the interviewees' report relationships with teachers that they find supportive and instrumental. Carl, a year 11 student, compares the way in which work experience is framed, reviewed and supported in the Centre as opposed to school:

> Carl: ...and just go there [work experience] and come back [to school] with, um, your letter. But, like, at here they're like talking about it to you and that. Or like what opportunities you could do, you know.

Carl describes his work experience through the Centre in the context of future opportunities. Centre staff invest time into making work experience meaningful and a potential foundation for future employment. I saw Carl in the summer term after the interview and learned that he had earned a place on a Catering Modern Apprenticeship scheme. This may not be directly attributable to the Centre, but their commitment to Careers Guidance and quality work experience almost certainly played a role and the relationship between Carl and institutional agents illustrates the model advocated by Stanton-Salazar.

The key to the Centre approach seems to be that teachers *value* young people on an interpersonal level and show it by interacting respectfully, putting time and effort into personal relationships with students, providing real opportunities to learn and the help students feel they need to achieve in the Centre and beyond. Yet the teacher-student relationship so central to the experiences of the young people in this study barely features in the present School Effectiveness and Improvement movement. Newspaper reports of discussions around League Tables and target-setting, effective subject teaching, and performance-related pay say little about the quality of teacher-student relationships and what might foster or impede positive relations. Disregard of this key issue prevails, despite ample evidence from students that the relationship with teachers is the feature of their educational experience that matters most (e.g. Wallace, 1996; Garner, 1995; Wright, 1993).

Some schools have introduced initiatives that recognise the significance of positive relationships with adults, particularly for the most disaffected young people. Tim Brighouse, Chief Education Officer for Birmingham, cites the example of one school's efforts to reduce exclusion through promoting positive teacher-student relationships. The teachers identified

25 young people in year 7 who they predicted would be excluded by the end of the next year and then each teacher undertook to speak to one allocated young person in the corridor every day. By the end of year 8, none of the named 25 young people had been excluded (*Guardian*, 14-9-1999). This example shows how a fairly straightforward and easily implemented policy can have a massive impact on young people's experience of school. It also supports the claim made here that the relationship between teachers and students is a hugely powerful shaper of students' experiences.

A Yorkshire pilot programme that aimed to establish positive adult-student relationships provides another example. Support workers were placed in schools to befriend students, work with them on anger management and try to improve their self-esteem and their peer relationships. The University of York researchers evaluating the programme report that: '...in four of the five schools so far examined, the involvement of the support worker is seen as greatly reducing the number of exclusions, particularly fixed-term ones' (*TES*, 8-10-99, p.33). Again we see the power of a positive adult-young person relationship. It is easy to imagine that such initiatives might have benefited the young people in this study.

These positive relationships together address every area of difficulty experienced by the young people in this study. To befriend the young people, the support staff had to make some connection with them and establish rapport – and this would have meant listening to what they had to say about their lives at school. Making time for listening would have been an integral part of their brief. We know that not being listened to is a common complaint of young people and that it leaves them feeling undervalued and uncared for. Listening is only a first step, however, and could stop short of providing young people with the support they need to remain in school. The support workers in the Yorkshire scheme taught young people about anger management. Managing anger was another key issue for students who described themselves as 'easy to wind up' or 'bad tempered' and for whom their temper would lead to fighting with peers and so get them into trouble with teachers. The ability to manage their anger effectively could have prevented much of the disruptive behaviour described by the interviewees.

Support workers in the Yorkshire schools addressed other concerns of students which again mirrored the concerns of the interviewees. They tried to improve the young people's self-esteem and their relationships with other students, which are such an important factor in the experience of school. These support workers apparently recognised this. They also offered advice '...on personal social and health problems, and helped to arrange out-of-school leisure activities' (p.33), so provided guidance and support for students facing such difficulties.

However, individual positive relationships are not enough in themselves to make schools fully inclusive. In this study, several young people des-cribed extremely positive relationships with individual teachers and yet their overall experience of school was largely negative and they were still excluded. For positive relationships to have far-reaching benefits, they need to be set within a supportive whole-school environment. In the Yorkshire study, the support workers were seen to help 'develop a school ethos which is more tolerant and supportive of such pupils' (p.3). In-clusion must be tackled on a whole-school, systemic level to be truly effective.

The BSS Centres 'worked' as learning environments for the young people in the study because they did not feel as though they were valued differentially. 'Success' was defined much more broadly and so allowed much more scope for feeling 'successful'. Young people enjoyed friendly, less formal relationships with Centre teachers and, more that that, instrumental interactions. The students in the Centres were given relevant academic and careers advice and opportunities to explore career options and plan their post-16 experiences. The Centre structure certainly makes it easier for staff to establish the kinds of relationships with students that seem to benefit them most.

This should not mean that schools cannot create a learning environment where all young people feel valued and that their needs are met. Steps can be taken to create an environment that fosters the kinds of relation-ships and instrumental dialogues that characterise the Centres and the Yorkshire schools. One problem lies in schools being social systems in which each student's value and status is determined by the teaching staff – who award status predominantly for academic performance and good behaviour, in line with the dominant discourse. The views of young people, particularly those of low status, had no part in this discourse and their 'voices' were seldom heard and were excluded from the formal school culture. So these students felt apart from this culture – excluded from it before they were permanently excluded from school.

For the social system to become inclusive of all students power has to be shared. The observations of Cummins (1994) about the nature of power relations with regard to literacy instruction are applicable to education generally: 'literacy instruction is always either an element of coercive relations of power or alternatively part of a challenge to the power structure...' (p.325). The caring, supportive relationships that so enhance students' experience in the Centres result from power relations that differ from those described in mainstream schools. The Centres have altered the dominant school discourse, particularly by broadening the criteria for what is valuable, so that the abilities and efforts of a greater number of students are valued. 'Valuing' students and their skills serves to shift the restrictive boundaries that limit their potential for a positive educational experience. The Centres create more opportunity to succeed – both opportunity that is tangible, such as work experience, and that which is more abstract, such as an atmosphere that fosters an increasingly positive sense of self-worth.

Centre teachers have a disproportionate share of power within the institution, just as teachers in mainstream school do. But Centre teachers use their power differently. They are more responsive to their students, as this example shows. At one Centre I visited, the students had told staff that they objected to groups being named 'A-group', 'B-group', etc. because of the connotations of worth and hierarchy. The staff renamed the groups according to the first letter of the teacher's name (K-group, S-group, G-group). Clearly they listened to the students' concerns, took them seriously, and acted on them. However, the decision to recognise that the issue of group-names was a 'problem' and determine a solution came from the teaching staff. Moves to incorporate the student voice into school policy – in Centres and especially in mainstream schools – could go further.

Cummins (1994) identifies two distinct types of power relations: coercive and cooperative. The first – the exercise of power by the dominant group to the detriment of a subordinate group – assumes that power exists in a fixed quantity. It defines the subordinate group as inferior, necessarily making the dominant group superior, in order to justify greater power. Where power relations are collaborative, power is not fixed but can be generated by interpersonal relations; it is created in the relationship and shared among participants (p.299). The Centres approximate to collaborative relations of power by hearing and regarding the student voice, and by valuing a greater range of knowledge and skills in their students.

Michael Fielding (1997) takes collaborative education one step further with his vision of 'transformative education'. Fielding developed this concept in response to his dissatisfaction with the School Effectiveness and Improvement Movement, and the work in his school that involved students in research into issues of quality in the education it provided. Fielding views education as a key element in developing a democratic society (p.154) and his notions of transformative education embrace student involvement as part of daily life, on issues affecting the working life of both students and adults. Not only is the individual teacher required to engage with young people in discussion, but so is the entire institution. And the institution is also required to equip students with the intellectual and process skills to inquire into the nature of their educational experience (p.153-154).

Fielding shows how practice that engages young people and incorporates their views into policy and practice is feasible in a large mainstream school and not only in small Centres. At Sharnbrook Upper School and Community College, Fielding and his colleagues actively engaged students in the school improvement process (see Jackson *et al.*, 1998, for a full account). Students were trained in research techniques and formed research groups to study issues relevant to themselves and the school generally, including profiling and assessment, student involvement and the preparation of student teachers. The student-researchers worked alongside teaching staff and school officials and their findings were integrated into the School Improvement policy. Power is shared. Young people help to define what the 'issues' are in the school, participate actively in exploring those issues and contribute to proposals for change.

Fielding (1997) demonstrates that engaging students in discussion and incorporating their views into practice, as in the Centres, can also be done in mainstream school. This is one way that the young people's positive experiences in the Centres can inform mainstream practice. Fielding also identifies a need to develop the inclusion of student views in a way that ensures students are equipped with the tools they need to guide their own learning, including inquiring into the nature of this learning. We saw the students in this study questioning one aspect of their learning environment in the Centres – how groups were named – but this is a relatively isolated incident. Fielding's model goes beyond isolated incidents; he calls for a system in which 'the process of involving students was seen as part of the normal way in which a school goes about its daily work' (p.153). Such a level of student involvement over a wide range of issues, with the implicit aim of helping young people to shape their own learning, was not reflected in the interviewees' accounts of their experiences at the Centres, and still less at school. Neither does it seem to be implied in the emerging work on the citizenship curriculum that will become mandatory for schools in 2002 (*TES*, 26-2-1999). Yet this approach is compatible with the interviewees' expressed needs to be heard, taken seriously, and generally treated more like adults.

Power sharing does not mean teachers give up their power. Their responsibilities as educators and pastoral carers continue. But they would use their power and responsibility differently: to create space for young people to express and explore their views on a wide array of issues relevant to their daily lives. Teachers would use their power and creativity to develop a means for ensuring that young people's voices are heard within the formal school culture and that these voices are included among those that count in decision-making processes. When young people's voices, views and experiences begin to count in the formal school culture, young people become a part of that culture. For inclusion to be a realistic aim, the power held by the institutional agents of education must be shared with the student population – and that means all members of that population. There must be room within the formal school culture to recognise, value and integrate the informal school culture that is created by young people. Although positive interpersonal relationships are essential, inclusion must occur at the level of cultural rather than individual inclusion in order to be successful.

The conclusions emerging here are derived from the views of thirty-three young men and women permanently excluded from school. They are predominantly working-class, from a variety of ethnic backgrounds and a relatively large number of secondary schools in one city. Although few in number, the issues raised by their accounts relating to power relations within the school, the nature of the dominant discourse and how borders created by the discourse serve to de-legitimise the voices of low-status youth, are widely applicable. The implications of this work for policy and practice demand re-thinking power relations in schools and the nature of students' involvement in individual decisions such as those relating to specific disciplinary incidents, and in school-wide concerns such as those outlined by Jackson *et al.* (1998). However, students are only one of several key 'stakeholders' in the education system, as Nieto (1994) points out:

> Nobody has all the answers, and suggesting that students' views should be adopted wholesale is to accept a romantic view of students that is just as partial and condescending as excluding them completely from the discussion. (Nieto, 1994, p.398)

My argument is not that the students alone should determine policy and practice, merely that the inclusion of student voices on educational matters is beneficial in several ways: it provides us with direct feedback on the effect of particular policies-in-practice and also with an insight into the formal and informal cultures that so affect young people's experience of school. And the act of incorporating young people's views is beneficial to the young people themselves, helping them to feel valued and legitimising their voices.

Institutionalising students' involvement would engage young people and reduce disaffection. The restrictive borders that limit some young people's potential for experiencing school positively are constructed when their knowledge, skills and experiences are not valued as part of the dominant discourse. Valuing young people's views, especially for low-status youth, and incorporating them into policy decision-making would automatically legitimise the voice of these young people within the dominant discourse. But power relations within school would need to shift considerably before students views gained greater status. As Cummins (1994) points out, this does not mean teachers losing power, but rather power being generated collaboratively through interpersonal relationships. As power relations shift, the nature of the school discourse will also change, to embrace a wider range of knowledge, skills and experiences. When the views of students – all students – contribute to policy decisions that affect the working practices of teachers and school administrators, then young people can know that their views are truly valued and their voice unquestionably legitimate. Only then will the discourse of school include and not exclude young people.

Bibliography

BCC (Birmingham City Council) (1995) Joint Report of Chief Education and Director of Social Services. *Exclusions – The Interim Report of a Working Party*

Bealing, V. (1990) Inside information: pupil perceptions of absenteeism in the secondary school, *Maladjustment and Therapeutic Education*, 8(1), pp.19-33

Becker, H. (1971) Social-class variations in the teacher-pupil relationship, in: The School and Society Course Team at the Open University, *School and Society: A sociological reader,* London, Routledge and Keegan Paul, pp.119-125

Blatchford, P. (1996) Pupils' views on school work and school from 7-16 years, *Research Papers in Education*, 11(3), pp. 263-288

Blyth, E. and Milner, J. (1993) Exclusion from school: a first step in exclusion from society? *Children and Society*, 7(3), pp. 255-268

Bridges, L. (1994) Exclusions: how did we get here? in: J. Bourne, L. Bridges, and C. Searle *Outcast England: How Schools Exclude Black Children*, London, Institute of Race Relations

BSS (Behaviour Support Service) (1997) *Management Summary – Permanent Exclusions*, 1994/95, 1995/96

Chaplain, R. (1996) Making a strategic withdrawal: disengagement and self-worth protection in male pupils, in: J. Rudduck, R. Chaplain, and G. Wallace, (eds.) *School Improvement: What Can Pupils Tell Us?* London, David Fulton

Cohen, R. and Hughes, M. (1994) *School's Out: The Family Perspective on School Exclusion*, London, Family Service Unit and Barnardo's

Cooper, P. (1992) 'Exploring Pupils' Perceptions of the Effects of Residential Schooling on Children with Emotional and Behavioural Difficulties'. *Therapeutic Care and Education*, 1, pp. 22-34

Cooper, P. (1993) Field relations and the problem of authenticity in researching participants' perceptions of teaching and learning in classrooms, *British Educational Research Journal*, 19(4), pp. 323-338

CRE (Commission for Racial Equality)(1997) *Exclusion from School and Racial Equality: A Good Practice Guide*, London, CRE

Crozier, J. and Antiss, J. (1995) Out of the spotlight: girls' experience of disruption, in: M. Lloyd-Smith and J. D. Davies (eds.) *On the Margins: The Educational Experience of 'Problem' Pupils*, Stoke on Trent, Trentham

Cullingford, C. and Morrision, J. (1995) Bullying as a formative influence: the relationship between the experience of school and criminality, *British Educational Research Journal*, 21(5), pp. 547-560

Cullingford, C. and Morrison, J. (1997) Peer pressure within and outside school, *British Educational Research Journal,* 23(1), pp. 61-80

Cummins, J. (1994) From coercive to collaborative relations of power in teaching literacy, in: B. Ferdman, R-M Weber, and A. Ramireq (eds.) *Literacy Across Languages and Cultures*, New York, State University of New York Press

Day, J. (1996) The reckoning, in: J. Rudduck, R. Chaplain, and G. Wallace (eds.) *School Improvement: What Can Pupils Tell Us?* London, David Fulton

Department for Education (1992) *Exclusions: a Discussion Paper,* London, DFE

de Pear, S. (1997) Excluded pupils' views of their educational needs and experiences, *Support for Learning,* 12(1), pp. 19-22

de Pear and Garner, P. (1996) Tales from the exclusion zone: the views of teachers and pupils, in: E. Blyth and J. Milner (eds.) *Exclusion from School,* London, Routledge

Elliott, J. (1996) School effectiveness research and its critics: alternative visions of school, *Cambridge Journal of Education,* 26(2), pp. 199-223

Elliott, J. (1998) *The Curriculum Experiment: Meeting the Challenge of Social Change,* Buckingham, Open University Press

Fielding, M. (1997) Beyond school effectiveness and school improvement: lighting the slow fuse of possibility, in: M. Barber and J. White (eds.) *Perspectives on School Effectiveness and School Improvement,* London, Bedford Way Papers

Final Report to the Department for Education: National survey of local education authorities policies and procedures for identification of, and provision for, children who are out of school by reason of exclusion or otherwise. (1995) Canterbury: Canterbury Christ Church College

Flavell, J., Miller, P., and Miller, S. (1993) *Cognitive Development,* 3rd edition, New Jersey, Prentice-Hall

Galloway, D. (1985) Persistent absence and exclusion in school: predictive power of school and community variables, *British Educational Research Journal,* 11(1), pp. 51-61

Gannaway, H. (1976) Making sense of school, reprinted in: M. Hammersley and P. Woods (eds.)(1984) *Life in School: The Sociology of Pupil Culture,* Buckingham, Open University Press, pp. 191-203

Garner, P. (1995) Schools by scoundrels: the views of 'disruptive' pupils in mainstream schools in England and the United States, in: M. Lloyd-Smith and J. D. Davies (eds.) *On the Margins: The Educational Experience of 'Problem' Pupils,* Stoke on Trent, Trentham

Gillborn, D. and Gipps, C. (1996) *Recent Research into the Achievement of Ethnic Minority Pupils,* London, HMSO

Giroux, H. (1989) *Schooling for Democracy: Critical Pedagogy in the Modern Age,* London, Routledge

Graham, J. and Bowling, B. (1995) *Young People and Crime,* London, Home Office.

The Guardian (14-9-1999) Beware the exclusion zone, Jan Parker

The Guardian (29-11-1996) Exclusions cost society £24m a year, Josephine Gardiner

The Guardian (26-11-1996) Damage Limitation, Peter Kingston

The Guardian (22-11-1996) Teachers 'partly to blame' for expulsion rise, Donald MacLeod

The Guardian (11-10-1996) 'Crisis' over black exclusion, Donald MacLeod

Hargreaves, D. (1967) *Social Relations in Secondary School*, London, Routledge and Keegan Paul

Hatcher, R. (1999) Social justice and the politics of school effectiveness and improvement, *Race, Ethnicity and Education*, 1(2), pp. 267-289

Howe, T. (1995) Former pupils' reflections on residential special provision, in: M. Lloyd-Smith and J. D. Davies (eds.) *On the Margins: The Educational Experience of 'Problem' Pupils*, Stoke on Trent, Trentham

Kinder, K., Wilkin, A. and Wakefield, A. (1997) *Exclusion: Who Needs It?* Slough, NFER

Lloyd-Smith, M. (ed)(1984) *Disrupted Schooling,* London, John Murray

Lloyd-Smith, M. and Davies, J. D. (1995) (eds.) *On the Margins: The Educational Experience of 'Problem' Pupils*, Stoke on Trent, Trentham

Lovey, J., Docking, J., and Evans, R. (1993) *Exclusion from School: Provisions for Disaffection in Key Stage 4*, London, David Fulton

Mac an Ghaill, M. (1993) Beyond the white norm: The use of qualitative methods in the study of black youths' schooling in England, in: P. Woods and M. Hammersley (eds.) *Gender and Ethnicity in Schools: Ethnographic Accounts*, London, Routledge

Mac an Ghaill, M. (1996) 'What about the boys': Schooling, class and crisis masculinity, *The Editorial Board of the Sociological Review*, pp. 381-397

McLean, A (1987) After the belt: school processes in low exclusion schools, *School Organization*, 7(3), pp. 303-310

McManus, M. (1987) Suspension and exclusion from high schools: the association with catchment and school variables, *Research in Education*, 38, pp. 51-63

Nieto, S. (1994) Lessons from students on creating a chance to dream, *Harvard Educational Review,* 64 (4), pp. 392-426

OFSTED (Office for Standards in Education) (1996) *Exclusions from Secondary School 1995/96,* London, OFSTED

OFSTED (1993) *Education for Disaffected Pupils*, London, OFSTED

O'Keefe, D. and Stoll, P. (eds.) (1995) *School Attendance and Truancy: Understanding and Managing the Problem,* London, Pitman

Parsons, C., Castle, F., Howlett, K., and Worrall, J. (1996) *Exclusion from School: The Public Cost,* London, CRE

Phelan, P., Cao, H. and Davidson, A. (1994) Navigating the psychosocial pressures of adolescence: the voices and experiences of high school youth, *American Educational Research Journal*, 31(2), pp. 415-447

Phelan, P., Davidson, A. and Yu, H. (1993) Students' multiple worlds: navigating the borders of family, peer and school cultures, in: P. Phelan and A. Davidson (eds.) *Renegotiating Cultural Diversity in American Schools*, New York, Columbia University Teachers' College Press

Price, J. and Dodge, K. (1989) Peers' contributions to children's social maladjustment, in: T.J. Berndt and G.W. Ladd (eds) *Peer Relationships in Child Development,* New York, Wiley

Reid, K. (1986) *Disaffection from School,* London, Metheuen

Reynolds, D. (1976) When pupils and teachers refuse a truce: the secondary school and the creation of delinquency, in: G. Mungham and G. Pearson (eds.) *Working Class Youth Culture,* London, Routledge and Kegan Paul

Reynolds, D. (1982) The search for effective schools, *School Organisation* 2(3), pp.215-237

Rudduck, J., Chaplain, R. and Wallace, G. (eds.)(1996) *School Improvement: What Can Pupils Tell Us?* London, David Fulton

Rutter, M., Maughan, B., Mortimore, P. and Ousten, J. (1979) *Fifteen Thousand Hours: Secondary Schools and Their Effect on Children*, London, Open Books

Sammons, P. and Reynolds, D. (1997) A partisan evaluation – John Elliott on school effectiveness, *Cambridge Journal of Education*, 27(1), pp. 123-136

Sewell, T. (1997) *Black Masculinities and Schooling: How Black Boys Survive Modern Schooling,* Stoke on Trent, Trentham

SHA (Secondary Heads Association) (1992) *Excluded from School: A Survey of Secondary School Exclusions*, Bristol, H.E. Iles

Sinclair-Taylor, A. (1995) A 'dunce's place': pupils' perceptions of the role of a special unit, in: M. Lloyd-Smith and J. D. Davies (eds.) *On the Margins: The Educational Experience of 'Problem' Pupils*, Stoke on Trent, Trentham

SooHoo, S. (1993) Students as partners in research and restructuring schools, *The Educational Forum,* 57, pp. 386-392

Stanton-Salazar, R. (1997) A social capital framework for understanding the socialization of racial minority children and youths, *Harvard Educational Review,* 67(1), pp. 1-41

Stirling, M. (1992) How many pupils are being excluded? *British Journal of Special Education,* 19(4), pp. 128-130

TES (Times Educational Supplement) (8-10-1999) Support staff 'slash' exclusions'

TES (5-3-99) Councils called in over black exclusions, Frances Rafferty and Karen Thornton

TES (26-2-1999) Citizenship smitten, Sarah Cassidy

TES (12-2-1999) Families hold the key, Masud Hoghughi

TES (10-4-1998) Call for rising exclusions to trigger inspections, Susan Young

TES (3-4-1998) Exclusions cost 2m days/year, Dorothy Lepkowska

TES (20-2-1998) Exclusions may lead to fines, says Labour, Geraldine Hackett

TES (10-10-97) Exclusions drama turns into a crisis for blacks, Audrey Osler

TES (26-9-1997) Exclusions 'spiral out of control'

Wallace, G. (1996) Relating to teachers, in: J. Rudduck, R. Chaplain, and G. Wallace (eds.) *School Improvement: What Can Pupils Tell Us?* London, David Fulton

Whyte, R. and Brockington, D. (1983) *Tales Out of School: Consumers Views of British Education.* London, Routledge and Keegan Paul

Willis, P (1977) *Learning to Labour: How Working Class Kids Get Working Class Jobs*, Westmead, Saxon House

Woods, P. (1990) *The Happiest Days? How Pupils Cope with School*, London, Falmer Press

Wright, C. (1993) School processes – an ethnographic study, in: P. Woods and M. Hammersley (eds.) *Gender and Ethnicity in Schools: Ethnographic Accounts,* London, Routledge

Wright, C., Weeks, D., McGlaughlin, A. and Webb, D. (1998) Masculinised discourses within education and the construction of black male identities amongst African-Caribbean youth, *British Journal of Sociology of Education*, 19, 1, pp. 75-87

Zeng, J.J. (1998) Race, cultural identity and gender: the researcher in the research process, *Research Intelligence*, 64, pp. 21-25

Index